# Comfort from the Bible

**TIMOTHY CROSS**

**AMBASSADOR**
Belfast • Greenville

*Comfort from the Bible*
© 1996 Timothy Cross

ISBN 1 898787 62 X

Published by

**AMBASSADOR PRODUCTIONS, LTD.**
Providence House
16 Hillview Avenue,
Belfast, BT5 6JR

Emerald House
1 Chick Springs Road, Suite 102
Greenville, South Carolina, 29609

# Contents

# Dedication

*With heartfelt thanks and praise to the one, true and living God, Who has promised in His Word that 'My grace is sufficient for you' (2 Corinthians 12:9).*

# Preface

A Minister friend once told me that "Christian ministry should disturb the comfortable and comfort the disturbed." This book is sent with a view to the latter, as over the years so many broken hearts in need of healing seem to have crossed my path. In the following pages I share with you some of the promises of God in the Bible that have been a great blessing and comfort to me over the past months - months which have certainly had their darker, trying moments.

'Comfort,' in the Bible, is somewhat different from the popular image of a rather weak 'tea and sympathy.' Biblical 'comfort' is a strong word. Comfort contains the word 'fort' in it, and is derived from the word 'encouragement,' which means 'to put courage in.' The Bible reveals that each member of the Tri-une Godhead is involved in the ministry of comfort:-

1. God the Father is 'the God of all *comfort* ' (2 Corinthians 1:3)
2. God the Son was sent to 'bind up the broken hearted and *comfort* all who mourn ' (Isaiah 61:1,2)
3. God the Holy Spirit's very name, in the Authorised Version, is translated as 'The *Comforter*' (John 14:16).

It is my hope and prayer that in reading these pages your experience of the comfort of God and the God of all comfort will be increased.

'Now may our Lord Jesus Christ Himself, and God our Father, Who loved us and gave us eternal *comfort* and good hope through grace, *comfort* your hearts and establish them in every good work and word' (2 Thessalonians 2:16,17).

**Timothy J.E. Cross**
*Cardiff, South Wales.*

# The Comfort of God's Pardon

*Blessed is he whose transgression is forgiven, whose sin is covered. Blessed is the man to whom the Lord imputes no iniquity (Psalm 32:1,2).*

Divine forgiveness is a supernatural source of comfort integral to the whole Christian Faith. The experience of Divine forgiveness is a Christian fundamental lying at the heart of genuine, biblical Christianity. Human nature is such that every human being is in desperate need of forgiveness if fellowship with God is ever to be attained and enjoyed both in this life and the next; and no book but the Bible can give the Divine assurance that if we belong to Christ, God has blotted out our transgressions and will not remember our sins (Isaiah 43:25).

## PSALM 32 : THE BACKGROUND

Psalm 32:1,2 are such comforting verses – but the events which caused King David to write them are most discomforting. 2 Samuel 11 and 12 is the ugly background which gave birth to this beautiful Psalm:–

David, the king who was raised so high, also fell very low. Giving into temptation he commited adultery with Bathsheba and in an attempt to cover up his sin engineered the death of her husband Uriah. No one sins and gets away with it – not even a king. 'Be sure your sin will find you out' (Numbers

32:23). God had commanded 'You shall not commit adultery' (Exodus 20:14), and this applied as much to King David as it did to the lowliest of his household servants. And so the Lord, through Nathan the prophet, convicted David of his heinous crime. David was so wracked with guilt that it even affected him physically. He records in this Psalm:- 'When I declared not my sin, my body wasted away through my groaning all day long ... my strength was dried up as by heat of summer' (Psalm 32:3,4). Mercifully for him though, the story did not end there, for 'David said to Nathan "I have sinned against the Lord." And Nathan said to David, "The Lord has put away your sin."' (2 Samuel 12:13). The unbearable load of guilt was then lifted away and floods of joy filled David's soul. To celebrate his release, he wrote this thirty second Psalm - and God has ensured that the Psalm has been kept for posterity.

The Psalm begins by extolling the blessedness of knowing God's forgiveness – and the Psalm ends on a similarly joyful note with the exhortation 'Be glad in the Lord, and rejoice, O righteous, and shout for joy, all you upright in heart' (Psalm 32: 10,11). David certainly was not righteous in and of himself – and neither are we. Righteousness means being in a right relationship with God, and this is only possible if He forgives our sins. It was the personal knowledge and experience that God does just that, which was the cause of David's joy. 'Thou dost forgive the guilt of my sin' (Psalm 32:5 ).

Having discussed something of the blessing of and the background to our text, let us now analyse it in further detail. Consider:-

## 1. THE CONDITION WHICH IS MAGNIFIED

'Blessed is he whose transgression is forgiven'. Blessed! Psalm 32:1 is a lesser known beatitude (compare this with Jesus's nine 'blesseds' in the Beatitudes with which He opens the 'Sermon on the Mount' (Matthew 5:3-11)). 'Blessed' could be paraphrased as 'Happy' or 'How happy' or 'Oh, the happiness of ... the one who knows God has forgiven all his sins.'

True blessed-ness is unattainable apart from the God Who imparts His blessing. God alone is, as the hymnwriter said, 'the fount of every blessing.' The fact that God blesses those who deserve nothing but His wrath, shows something of the graciousness of the Divine character. He is 'the God of all grace' (1 Peter 5:10) Who bestows the blessing of His forgiveness upon guilty sinners.

Proverbs 10:22 reads: 'The blessing of the Lord makes rich and He adds no sorrow with it.' The Apostle Paul, in New Testament times, thinking of the riches that God bestows on poor sinners, could only overflow with exuberant praise:– 'Blessed be the God and Father of our Lord Jesus Christ, Who has blessed us in Christ with every spiritual blessing in the heavenly places' (Ephesians 1:3). In enumerating these blessings, Paul too rejoices in God's forgiveness - God's forgiveness through Jesus Christ. He continues his praise by explaining 'In Him we have redemption through His blood, the forgiveness of our trespasses according to the riches of His grace which He lavished upon us' (Ephesians 1:7,8).

'Blessed', begins this thirty-second Psalm of Benediction. C.H. Spurgeon said of this blessed man of this Psalm:-

> 'He is now blessed, and ever shall be. Pardoning mercy is of all things in the world most to be prized, for it is the only sure way to happiness. Blessedness is not in this case ascribed to the man who has been a diligent lawkeeper, for then it would never come to us, but rather to a lawbreaker, who by grace most rich and free has been forgiven.'

## TRUE BLESSEDNESS

The world preaches that we need all sorts of things to be happy and blessed – money, health, holidays, sex... but the Bible implies here that to be truly blessed we need to know that our sins are forgiven.

David does not extol any old happiness here in Psalm 32, but rather the specific happiness of knowing that our 'transgressions' are forgiven. To transgress means 'to defy' or 'to rebel against lawful authority.' David certainly had done that in the infamous incident with Bathsheba – but God in His mercy forgave David his wrongdoing, and David rejoiced.

The word used for forgiveness here has the meaning of 'taking a heavy burden away.' God is able to act in this manner because of Christ, the Messiah to Whom David looked forward, and the Messiah to Whom we look back. Isaiah records of the Messiah 'He was wounded for our transgressions' (Isaiah 53:5) – wounded to take away from us our load of guilt. When the Holy Spirit makes this effectual in our hearts the comfort and joy is immeasurable. In the second best selling book of all time – Bunyan's *Pilgrim's Progress* – 'Christian', the main character also knew what it was to be bowed down with an unbearably heavy load of sin – but he too experienced a joyful release when he came to the cross of Jesus:–

> I saw in my dream that just as Christian came up with the cross, his burden loosed from off his shoulders, and fell off his back ... and I saw it no more. Then was Christian glad and lightsome– (when God releases us of our guilt and burden, we are as those who leap for joy.)... Then Christian gave three leaps for joy, and went out singing:-
>
> > *'Thus far did I come laden with my sin*
> > *Nor could I ought ease the grief that I was in*
> > *Till I came hither. What a place is this!*
> > *Must here be the beginning of my bliss?*
> > *Must here the burden fall from off my back?*
> > *Must here the strings that bound it to me crack?*
> > *Blest cross! Blest sepulchre! Blest rather be*
> > *The Man that there was put to death for me.'*

The forgiveness of sins through the death of Jesus Christ is a Christian basic - a basic to which we will have cause to return throughout our earthly lives. It is the forgiveness of sins through the finished work of Christ on the cross which alone gives us assurance and re-assurance. John, the beloved disciple, became a church leader and respected elder in his later years. In his first letter we might have expected him to expound some very profound theology. He certainly did. But he also states simply and reassuringly to his Christian readers 'I am writing to you little children because your sins are forgiven for His sake' (1 John 2:12). Such a reassurance will never get outdated in this life.

## 2. THE COVERING WHICH IS MADE

'Blessed is he ... whose sin is covered.' Transgression, we have seen, refers to rebelling against God. 'Sin', however refers to missing the mark and falling short of God's holy standard (compare Romans 3:23). Sin not only brings on an awful sentence, but also brings with it an awful shame – but in His great mercy God covers over our shame.

The word 'covered' here means 'atoned for.' The concept of blood atonement is central to the message of the Bible. A key verse of Scripture is Leviticus 17:11:- 'The life of the flesh is in the blood; and I have given it to you upon the altar to make atonement for your souls; for it is the blood that makes atonement by reason of the life.' Throughout the Bible we see God Himself providing a covering for sin, guilt and judgment:-

In the Garden of Eden, God provided a covering for Adam and Eve, atoning for their sin and shame. At the Flood, God covered Noah and his family in the Ark, saving them from the devastating judgment outside. The whole of the Old Testament in fact, gives many prefigurations and insights into The Atonement - the blood of Jesus shed at Calvary to atone for guilty sinners, sinners too ashamed to look God in the face.

*A debtor to mercy alone*
*of Covenant mercy I sing*
*nor fear with God's righteousness on*
*my person and offering to bring.*
*The terrors of law and of God*
*with me can have nothing to do*
*My Savour's obedience and blood*
*hide all my transgressions from view.*

Jesus's righteousness, put to our account, more than adequately covers the shame of our sin, just as God had promised:- 'Remove the filthy garments from him ... Behold I have taken your iniquity away from you, and I will clothe you with rich apparel' (Zechariah 3:4). The wonder of the Gospel is that sinners can exchange the filthy rags of sin for the spotless robe of

Christ's righteousness, so that all sinful blemishes are completely covered over in God's sight for time and eternity. Truly, plenteous grace with God is found, grace to cover all our sin. But David is not finished yet. He has a third way of describing to us the joy of God's pardon.

## 3. THE COUNTING WHICH IS MARVELLED

'Blessed is the man to whom the Lord imputes no iniquity. ' The third word David uses to describe the human plight is 'iniquity.' This refers to the dreadful twist in our nature, a twist and crookedness inherited from Adam. The joy is though that God does not impute our iniquity to us - instead He imputes it to Christ.

### IMPUTATION

To impute means 'to put to someone's account.' Our iniquity puts us infinitely in God's debt, and this debt is the most horrific debt of all. The wonder of the Gospel is however, that because of Christ, God is able to clear our debt completely, changing our account with him from the red to the black. In Christ, God has had mercy on poor, bankrupt sinners. In His great mercy He writes off our debt so that sin is not only covered but cancelled. 'Payment God cannot twice demand, first at my bleeding surety's hand and then again at mine.' '...having forgiven us all our trespasses, having cancelled the bond which stood against us with its legal demands; this He set aside, nailing it to the cross' (Colossians 2:13,14).

Interestingly, Paul quotes these very verses of Psalm 32:1,2 in Romans 4:8, except in Romans it is translated 'Blessed is the man to whom the Lord will not reckon his sin.' Here then that we see the ultimate source of David's blessing is none other than the Lord Jesus Christ, great David's Greater Son. G.B. Wilson comments:-

> It is particularly pertinent to Paul's purpose that the man
> whom David pronounced blessed is not the man who has
> good works put to his account 'but whose sins are not laid

to his account.' And the apostle ... interprets this non reckoning of sin as the positive imputation of righteousness... God's forgiveness necessarily implies the complete reinstatement of the sinner.

Psalm 32:1,2 then are foundational verses for this book of Bible-comfort. Biblical comfort begins with our knowing that our sins are forgiven for Jesus Christ's sake. The text extols with great exuberance the blessedness of sins forgiven. This is a Divine source of comfort which I trust is yours just as it was David's.

A so called 'Pauline Psalm' asks 'If Thou, O Lord, shouldst mark iniquities, Lord who could stand?' (Psalm 130:4). Who indeed? But the next verse reads 'But there is forgiveness with Thee that Thou mayest be feared' (Psalm 130:4). Praise God that there is forgiveness with Him, no matter what our background and previous failures may be. God's forgiveness though was at the infinite cost of His own dear Son. Jesus died so that our transgressions may be forgiven, our sins covered and our iniquity not put to our account. This blessedness flowing from His death none can measure. This alone is our comfort. Here alone lies the soul's true well being.

*My sin, O the bliss of this glorious thought!*
*My sin, not in part but the whole,*
*Is nailed to His cross, and I bear it no more*
*Praise the Lord, praise the Lord, O my soul!*

# The Comfort of God's Justification

*Since all have sinned and fall short of the glory of God they are justified by His grace as a gift through the redemption which is in Christ Jesus, Whom God put forward as a propitiation by His blood, to be received by faith* (Romans 3:25,26).

## 1. THE MEANING OF JUSTIFICATION

Justification is a legal term. It is an exceedingly tense moment when a judge pronounces his verdict - 'Guilty' or 'Not guilty.' Yet judgments meted out in earthly courts will pale into insignificance when compared with God's judgment. When the Day comes for us to stand before the court of heaven, God Himself will pronounce His verdict on us. His 'Guilty' will result in our eternal damnation; His 'Not guilty' will result in our eternal bliss.

Justification concerns God's pronouncement of 'Not guilty' on guilty sinners. This seeming paradox at first seems too good to be true, if not totally unbelievable. Unless we have understood and experienced its reality it will always seem, from the outside, like a total contradiction, for 'He who justifies the wicked and he who condemns the righteous are both alike an abomination to the Lord' (Proverbs 17:15). The Christian Gospel however proclaims that God has found a way to be just and at the same time to justify guilty sinners when they trust in Christ (c.f. Romans 3:26).

Justification then concerns our righteousness - being in a right relationship with God. A very good definition of it is found in the Westminster *Shorter Catechism* when it states:-

Justification is an act of God's free grace, wherein He pardoneth all our sins and accepteth us as righteous in His sight, only for the righteousness of Christ imputed to us, and received by faith alone (Q.33).

## 2. THE MODE OF JUSTIFICATION

'they are justified by His grace as a gift...'

This surely is music to the sinner's ear. Justification, according to this verse, is by God's grace not human graft: God's mercy not our merit. How relieved we may be at this if we know anything of our inner selves. In God's sight even 'our righteous deeds are like a polluted garment' (Isaiah 64:6). We could never achieve the requisite righteousness acceptable to God by our own devices, as our sinful nature ensures all that we do is tainted by sin. 'Can the Ethiopian change his skin or the leopard his spots? Then also you can do good who are accustomed to do evil' (Jeremiah 13:23). There is no hope for us at all apart from God's grace.

Biblically, the root cause of our justification is the grace of God and the God of grace. God's grace is His undeserved favour - His goodwill to the undeserving and ill deserving. It is 'everything for nothing to those who don't deserve anything' but His wrath.

Salvation by the sheer grace of God is the distinguishing mark of Biblical Christianity. In all other religions and 'isms', salvation is viewed in terms of human attainment and human achievement, rather than by God's free gift. The Bible has no sympathy at all with these 'works salvations'. Justification is, according to the Bible, *God's* work, and is His free, gratuitous and gracious gift. 'It is God Who justifies' (Romans 8:37), 'so that we might be justified by His grace' (Titus 3:7). 'But if it is by grace, it is no longer on the basis of works; otherwise grace would no longer be grace' (Romans 11:6).

*Grace, 'tis a charming sound*
*Harmonious to the ear*
*Heaven with the echo shall resound*
*And all the earth shall hear*

*Grace first contrived a way*
*To save rebellious man*
*And all the steps that grace display*
*Which drew the wondrous plan*

## 3. THE MAKING OF JUSTIFICATION

God does not justify us, as it were 'just like that.' Rather, He actually had to do something extraordinarily costly in order that justification could come to us so freely. Justification, says our verse, is 'through the redemption that is in Christ Jesus, Whom God put forward as a propitiation by His blood'. The making of justification then, takes us to the heart of the Christian Faith, namely to the Cross of the Lord Jesus Christ. We are only, and can ever only be justified on the basis of the finished Work of Christ on Calvary's cross. Notice that Paul here uses two key words to explain the blessings of the cross:-

### i. Redemption

Redemption means 'freedom' – and so we can see how this ties in with being acquitted. When a judge makes the pronouncement 'Not guilty', the one on trial in the court goes free. Biblically, 'to redeem' means 'to set free by the paying of a price.' The picture is that of our being condemned to eternal death, awaiting our sentence, and then Christ coming along and setting us free. He sets us free because He has actually served our sentence for us, by dying our death penalty in our place. On this the Bible is crystal clear:- 'sending His Own Son in the likeness of sinful flesh and for sin, He condemned sin in the flesh, in order that the just requirement of the law might be fulfilled in us ...' (Romans 8:3,4). Jesus sets us free from sin's condemnation. He 'buys us out' with His blood. 'In Him we have redemption through His blood, the forgiveness of our trespasses according to the riches of His grace' (Ephesians 1:7). It is Jesus alone Who brings this eternal, spiritual freedom. 'If the Son makes you free you will be free indeed' (John 8:36).

## ii. Propitiation

'Propitiation by His blood'

The whole of the Christian Gospel is condensed in these four words. God the just law giver is rightly angered at every sinner who breaks His law. Our sin renders us guilty and deserving of punishment. Sin is a flout to God's authority and an affront to His majesty. The wrath of God is the most terrible reality ensuing from this. But the Gospel of propitiation refers to the merciful and gracious appeasement and satisfaction of God's wrath. GB Wilson comments:-

> The heart of the Gospel is that on the Cross God publically set forth Christ as a 'Propitiary offering' i.e. as the appointed means by which God's wrath against sinners is averted... Paul ... points every convicted sinner to the one sacrifice which satisfied the claims of Divine justice. The dreadful reality of God's wrath against sin required appeasement, but the magnitude of God's love was manifested in the very propitiation which sin demanded... Faith must find its pardon in Christ's sufferings for the guilty. For there can be no pacification of man's conscience apart from a believing interest in the blood which pacified God's wrath.

Christ then, is able to acquit the guilty but believing sinner, as on the cross He bore the awful punishment due to the sinner. In doing so He averted the wrath of God which is our due. 'He is the propitiation for our sins' (1 John 2:2). The love of God found a way in which to condemn sin and pardon the sinner – but at what cost. 'In this is love, not that we loved God but that He loved us and sent His Son to be the propitiation for our sins' (1 John 4:10).

Knowing that if we are 'in Christ' we will never be condemned for our sins is a great source and resource of comfort and confidence. 'There is therefore now no condemnation for those who are in Christ Jesus' (Romans 8:1). It is the cross of Christ which ensures that this is literally the Gospel truth.

There is no other Gospel and no other way of justification. Any other way nullifies God's grace and suggests that the cross was unnecessary:- 'I do not nullify the grace of God; for if justification were through the law, then Christ died to no purpose' (Galatians 2:21).

> *Jehovah bade His sword awake*
> *O Christ, it woke 'gainst Thee*
> *Thy blood the flaming blade must slake*
> *Thy heart its sheath must be*
> *All for my sake, my peace to make*
> *Now sleeps that sword for me*

## 4. THE MEANS OF JUSTIFICATION

' . . . to be received by faith.'

The Bible describes the same reality of justification in different ways and from different angles. For instance, it relates how we are justified by God's grace; we are justified by Christ's blood and we are also, it says here, justified by faith. These are all complementary as opposed to contradictory truths.

Faith is the means by which we receive and claim the saving benefits of Christ for ourselves. We could say that 'faith is an appropriation of His propitiation.' 'Propitiation does not take place except through faith on the part of the saved, and through blood on the part of the Saviour.' (Godet). All this follows most logically and 'theo-logically.' As justification is God's gracious gift through Christ, it can only, like all gifts, be received with gratitude. We have nothing at all to contribute except our sense of need. 'Nothing in my hands I bring, simply to the cross I cling'.

A motto passed down from the Protestant Reformation encapsulates the means of justification fully. This motto is 'Sola Gratia, Sola Fide, Sola Christus'; 'Grace alone, faith alone and Christ alone'. Question 85 of the *Shorter Catechism* is answered 'To escape the wrath and curse of God due to us for sin, God requireth of us faith in Jesus Christ.' Q.86 then asks 'What is faith in Jesus Christ?' and replies 'Faith in Jesus Christ is a saving grace, whereby we receive and rest upon Him alone for salvation, as He is offered to us in the Gospel.'

Our faith does not save us as such, rather it should be considered as the human channel through which we receive God's salvation; and yet even our faith is a gift of God. Merit is excluded totally. Ephesians 2:8,9 clarifies:- 'By grace you have been saved through faith, and this is not your own doing, it is the gift of God, not because of works, lest any man should boast.' Justification humbles us like nothing else. 'What have you that you did not receive?' (1 Corinthians 4:7).

> *Naught have I gotten, but I have received*
> *Grace has bestowed it, and I have believed*
> *Boasting excluded, pride I abase*
> *I'm only a sinner saved by grace.*

## 5. THE MARVEL OF JUSTIFICATION

Justification seems too good to be true. Such a salvation could never have been devised by man. No mere human could have devised a way for a holy God to declare guilty sinners righteous. Humanly speaking, it would seem impossible for God to find a way to be just and to justify sinners without compromising either the love or the justice integral to His nature. Yet such a way was found at the Cross of Calvary, in the person of Christ our Saviour-substitute. At the Cross God's justice and mercy met, condemning sin and pardoning the sinner. 'Steadfast love and faithfulness will meet; righteousness and peace will kiss each other' (Psalm 85:10).

Justification by faith is God's way of salvation, and God's way is perfect and sure. If justification by faith is a distinctively Protestant doctrine, then Jesus was a Protestant! In Luke 18:9 ff He told a parable that was to become famous. The parable is concerned with a 'good' man who went to hell and a 'bad' man who went to heaven. The good man went to hell because he tried to weave his own righteousness on the loom of his own good works; but the bad man simply admitted that he was an undeserving sinner, and casting himself on God cried 'God be merciful to me a sinner' (Luke 18:13). Jesus forced the point of the parable home by concluding 'I tell you, this man (i.e. the bad man) went down to his house justified rather than the other.'

Justification by faith, being God's way of salvation, is part of the very warp and woof of Scripture. This was Paul's Gospel. This is the Gospel of our Lord Jesus Christ. This was the Gospel of Israel's greatest earthly king - 'So also David pronounces a blessing upon the man to whom God reckons righteousness apart from works' (Romans 4:6). Abraham likewise, the great founding father of the Hebrew race, was saved by faith in God - 'Thus Abraham believed God and it was reckoned to him as righteousness' (Galatians 3:6). Habakkuk the prophet too, in a verse often quoted in the New Testament, taught 'the righteous shall live by his faith' (Habakkuk 2:4), and in the crowning prophecy of the Old Testament we also have the promise that 'by His knowledge shall the righteous One, My servant, make many to be accounted righteous' (Isaiah 53:11).

Justification by faith constitutes a major portion of the comfort that the Bible brings the believing soul. Since the Protestant Reformation, justification has been seen as *the* distinguishing mark whose presence or absence determines either a standing or a falling church. The doctrine is central to biblical theology, and yet such theology is no dry as dust, purely academic affair, but vital to the soul's true well-being. Justification is essential if we are to know ease of heart and mind in this life and the next. Indeed, Rev Edward Donelly went as far as to say 'If my people believed in justification by faith then 90 per cent of my pastoral problems would be solved.' Article XI of the *39 Articles* of the Church of England takes a similar view:

> We are accounted righteous before God, only for the merit of our Lord and Saviour Jesus Christ by faith, and not for our own works or deservings: Wherefore, *that we are justified by faith only is a most wholesome doctrine, and very full of comfort...*

# The Comfort of God's Adoption

*See what love the Father has given us, that we should be*
*called the children of God; and so we are*
**(1 John 3:1).**

If any doctrine in the Bible is practical, it is the doctrine of adoption. A true understanding of adoption is immensely comforting in the true sense of the word, making for both confident living and confident dying. Also, in understanding divine adoption, our love and adoration of the One Who has given us such a blessing will surely grow and flourish. Adoption fuels our worship – especially when we also realise how unworthy of such a blessing we are. Adoption, rightly considered, is the ideal environment for happiness, contentment and confidence to grow, secure under the protection of an all-powerful and all-loving heavenly Father.

## DEFINITIONS

Before we continue, let us have a precise definition of this blessed subject of adoption. The *Shorter Catechism* in Question 34 defines:-

Adoption is an act of free grace, whereby we are received
into the number and have a right to all the privileges of the
sons of God.

The *Westminster Confession* is fuller, and states in Chapter XII:-

> All those that are justified, God vouchsafeth, in and for His only Son Jesus Christ, to make partakers of the grace of adoption, by which they are taken into the number, and enjoy the liberties and privileges of the children of God, have His name put upon them, receive the spirit of adoption, have access to the throne of grace with boldness, are enabled to cry Abba, Father, are pitied, protected, provided for, and chastened by Him, as by a Father: yet never cast off, but sealed to the day of redemption; and inherit the promises, as heirs of salvation.

*O how shall I the goodness tell*
*Father, which Thou to me hast showed?*
*That I, a child of wrath and hell*
*I should be called a child of God*
*Should know, should feel my sins forgiven*
*Blest with this antepast of heaven!*

## 1. THE WAY OF ADOPTION

Adoption is not a blessing which comes naturally, but a blessing which is imparted supernaturally. It does not come by virtue of our being born (even if we are born into a Christian family) but by virtue of our being born-again. 'Regeneration' is the technical term here. Biblically, it is just not true that God is the Father of us all and we are all children of God. The Bible is plain when it declares us all 'dead through ... trespasses and sins... by nature children of wrath, like the rest of mankind' (Ephesians 2:2,3). It is only when God Himself gives us new spiritual life and in so doing brings us into His family that we become members of 'the household of God' (1 Timothy 3:15) or 'the household of Faith' (Galatians 6:10). Being by nature spiritually dead, we cannot bring new life to our own souls and so bring ourselves into God's family. Only God can do that. 'He saved us, not because of deeds done by us in righteousness, but in virtue of His Own mercy, by the washing of regeneration and renewal in the Holy Spirit' (Titus 3:5).

In a day of liberal, universalistic theology, it cannot be stressed too strongly that knowing God in an intimate child-Father relationship is a blessing only enjoyed by those who belong to Jesus Christ. Scripture is unequivocal:- 'to all who received Him, who believed in His name, He gave power to become children of God; who were born, not of blood nor of the will of the flesh nor of the will of man, but of God' (John 1:12,13).

As in justification, so with adoption, personal faith is the key which opens the door to our adoptive blessings:- 'For in Christ Jesus you are all sons of God, through faith '(Galatians 3:26). Jesus, of course, is the unique and eternally begotten Son of God. Our adoption only comes by our faith union with Him. 'Every one who believes that Jesus is the Christ is a child of God' (1 John 5:1). G.B. Wilson summed this up very nicely when he wrote:- 'He Who was the Son by nature willingly took the form of a servant, so that we who were by nature the servants of sin might become sons by the adoption of grace!'

Having laid these foundations - and pointed out some important riders - let us now consider something of:-

## 2. THE WONDER OF ADOPTION

As God's adopted children, it is our priceless privilege to revel in His fatherly affection, enjoy His fatherly fellowship, submit to His loving authority - knowing that He does all things well - and honour His fatherly majesty. A meditation on our new-birth rights is most heart-warming. God really does bring rebels into His household and lavish His love upon them. The Bible tells us so!

An illustration of the grace of adoption can be glimpsed in Mephibosheth, a lesser known character of the Old Testament. Mephibosheth's story is related in 2 Samuel 9, he was one of the late king Saul's sons. Mephibosheth was underprivileged in that 'he was lame in both feet' (2 Samuel 9:8) and if 2 Samuel 9:8 is anything to go by, rather low in self esteem. Yet this same Mephibosheth came under the favour of the king - the highest authority in the land. 'A king's ... favour is like dew upon the grass' (Proverbs 19:12). King David said to him 'I will show you kindness ... you shall eat at my table always' (2 Samuel 9:7), and sure enough, the account concludes 'So Mephibosheth dwelt in Jerusalem; for he ate always at the king's table' (2 Samuel 9:13). Unworthy as he was then, Mephibosheth was taken into the king's household and treated like a prince. This however is nothing in comparison with what God, through David's Greater Son has done and will do for the Christian. He has taken those of us who are Christ's into His Divine household. One day we will indeed sit at His table. 'Blessed are those who are invited to the marriage supper of the Lamb' (Revelation 19:9).

The privileges, blessings, benefits and comfort of divine adoption are immeasurable. We will consider just three of them:-

## i. TALKING TO OUR FATHER

It is on the basis of our adoption by God, into His family, through Christ, that we can be confident that we can take all our needs to Him in prayer, just as an earthly child comes to his father. Ole Hallesby defined prayer as 'Spreading out our helplessness before God.' To pray is to be dependant and we are all so dependant upon God, perhaps more than we realise. Knowing God as our Father gives us great incentive and confidence to pray, coming humbly as a child and spreading out our needs before Him.

According to Jesus, the secret of prayer is prayer in secret. But notice to Whom He encourages us to pray in secret:- 'When you pray, go into your room and shut the door and pray to your *Father* Who is in secret; and your *Father* Who sees in secret will reward you ' (Matthew 6:6).

When we pray, we may be assured of God's Fatherly kindness and undivided attention no matter how great or how small is our need. Indeed, His loving omniscience ensures that He knows our needs better than we do ourselves. 'Your heavenly Father knows what you need before you ask Him' (Matthew 6:8).

Jesus emphasised God's abounding kindness in relation to our prayers by way of contrast. It is unlikely that even an earthly father would refuse a legitimate request from his child - how inconceivable then that our heavenly

Father would refuse one from us. Says Jesus:- 'What father among you, if his son asks for a fish, will instead of a fish give him a serpent; or if he asks for an egg will give him a scorpion?' (Luke 11:11,12). 'If you then, who are evil, know how to give good gifts to your children, how much more will your Father in heaven give good things to those who ask Him!' (Matthew 7:11).

Prayer is instinctive to the Christian. One of the consequences of our new birth and adoption is that we talk to our Father in heaven. When Paul was first saved, it was said of him 'Behold, he is praying' (Acts 9:11). The same Paul could write later 'Because you are sons, God has sent the Spirit of His Son into our hearts crying "Abba! Father!"' (Galatians 4:6). Our adoption therefore means that we are actually on speaking terms with our God, Father and King. It is all too easy amongst the busy-ness of this world to neglect this means of grace, and not exploit it as much as we should or as much as we may.

> *Thou art coming to a King*
> *Large petitions with thee bring*
> *For His grace and power are such*
> *None can ever ask too much*

## ii. OUR TESTIMONY OF FAITH

Our adoption by God gives us the great and comforting assurance that all is eternally well with our souls. 'When we cry "Abba! Father!" it is the Spirit Himself bearing witness with our spirit that we are children of God' (Romans 8:15,16). Having been brought into God's family at the expense of His Son, it is as inconceivable as it is ludicrous to even suggest that God would ever cast us out. God Himself says:- 'Can a woman forget her sucking child, that she should have no compassion on the son of her womb? Even these may forget, yet I will not forget you. Behold, I have graven you on the palms of My hands' (Isaiah 49:16).

The Holy Spirit of God testifies to our eternal security in the Word He caused to be written. God's Word promises that if we are in Christ, we are both saved and safe. In Christ, through our new birth, 'we have the hope of eternal life which God, Who never lies, promised ages ago' (Titus 1:2). With confidence we may we sing:-

> *Blessed assurance Jesus is mine!*
> *O what a foretaste of glory Divine!*
> *Heir of salvation, purchase of God*
> *Born of His Spirit, washed in His blood.*

This leads us nicely to a third blessing of adoption, and that is:-

### iii. OUR TREASURE IN THE FUTURE

As the adopted children of God, our future is brighter and greater than we can ever conceive. Consider what John says in the next verse after our opening verse: 'Beloved, we are God's children now; it does not yet appear what we shall be...' (1 John 3:2).

In Biblical times at any rate, a child would inherit his father's estate. We, as children of God, are to inherit our heavenly Father's glory. Scripture is full of such promises, for instance:-

> 'So through God you are no longer a slave but a son, and if a son then an heir' (Galatians 4:7)
> 'we are children of God, and if children, then heirs, heirs of God and joint heirs with Christ' (Romans 8:17).
> 'justified by His grace and ... heirs in hope of eternal life' (Titus 3:7).

And so the blessings of our adoption are manifold now - and yet the best is yet to be. If we are Christians, we are saved now, but not wholly so. We all know the aches and pains of life in the body. One day, however, we will be saved bodily as well as spiritually, and enjoy full adoption in paradise restored. 'We wait for adoption of sons, the redemption of our bodies' (Romans 8:23). For this we have to wait for the Last Day, when our Saviour 'will change our lowly body to be like His glorious body, by the power which enables Him even to subject all things to Himself' (Philippians 3:21), gaining us a redeemed body for a redeemed earth.

There can be no higher blessing, privilege and comfort than divine adoption. Divine adoption brings us into God's family. It enables us to call God 'Father' and our fellow Christians 'brother' and 'sister'. It also assures us of a home in glory, where we will delight in our Father's presence for all eternity without let or hindrance. Then 'the house of Jacob shall possess their own possessions' (Obadiah 17).

*Behold the amazing gift of love*
*The Father has bestowed*
*On us the sinful sons of men*
*To call the sons of God*

*High is the rank we now possess*
*But higher we shall rise*
*Though what we shall hereafter be*
*Is hid from mortal eyes*

*A hope so great and so divine*
*May trials well endure*
*And purge the soul from sense and sin*
*As Christ Himself is pure.*

# Biblical Comfort For The Depressed

*Who among you fears the Lord and obeys the voice of His
servant, who walks in darkness and has no night, yet trusts
in the name of the Lord and relies upon His God?*
**(Isaiah 50:10).**

Depression of mind is a common but crippling ailment. The nature of this
debilitating mental illness is such that it is pushed somewhat underground.
It can come as something of a surprise therefore to see that the Bible has
much to offer by way of comfort to those locked in this darkest of dungeons.

## 1. THE BIBLE RECOGNISES THE DARKNESS OF DEPRESSION

Whilst modern soap operas portray something of an idealised, romanti-
cised world-view, Bible characters are painted 'warts and all.' When we realise that even great Bible characters got depressed, there is a solidarity in
suffering and we realise that are not so abnormal after all.

An unknown Psalmist, in Psalm 42, aware of better, brighter days, spoke
to himself. All depressives will be able to relate to the question he asked his
own soul:- 'Why are you cast down, O my soul, and why are you disquieted
within me?' (Psalm 42:5). What is depression if it is not being totally cast
down and downcast? The Psalmist though continued with the exhortation:
'Hope in God; for I shall again praise Him, my help and my God.' In a nut-
shell, that is the universal cure for spiritual depression. Depression turns us

inwards upon ourselves. Looking up and out to God however changes things. The awareness of His love and grace makes the world of difference. No matter how we feel, the depressed Psalmist assures us 'By day the Lord commands His steadfast love; and at night His song is with me' (Psalm 42:8). Spiritualising another Psalm, we too can say of our God, even in our most depressed and darkest moments 'even the darkness is not dark to Thee, the night is bright as the day; for darkness is as light with Thee' (Psalm 139:12).

The Bible then, the Book which shows us the road to heaven, certainly does not gloss over the hardships of earth, with its trials, troubles, disappointments and depression. Depression is one of the most subtle of hardships, as it is so real and yet so unseen. The Bible says 'No temptation (testing) has overtaken you that is not common to man' (1 Corinthians 10:13), and in another context 'the same experience of suffering is required of your brotherhood throughout the world' (1 Peter 5:9). No one is therefore immune from depression. This being so, let us view a few Biblical case-studies, and see how even the 'spiritual giants' also succumbed to this modern malady.

### i.  Jeremiah

Jeremiah was a most faithful prophet of God. A certain school of thought would have us think that personal blessing is directly commensurate with personal obedience. Jeremiah gives the lie to this  damaging assumption. Jeremiah was chosen by God for his life-work before he was born (Jeremiah 1:5); yet despite this evidence of Divine favour, he was not immune from life in the depths. In one of his blacker moments he groaned:-

'Cursed by the day on which I was born! The day when my mother bore me, let it not be blessed! Cursed by the men who brought the news to my father, "A son is born to you," making him very glad. Let that man be like the cities which the Lord overthrew without pity; let him hear a cry in the morning and an alarm at noon, because he did not kill me in the womb; so my mother would have been my grave, and her womb for ever great. Why did I come forth from the womb to see toil and sorrow, and spend my days in shame?' (Jeremiah 20:14-18).

At this particular moment, Jeremiah was so low that he wished he had never been born. Depression has such an effect on a person. Elsewhere in his writings however, Jeremiah helps us to take heart. He encourages us with the truth that God still sees and hears us no matter how low we get. In perhaps the saddest book of the Bible – Jeremiah's Lamentations – Jeremiah wrote these words:- 'I called on Thy name, O Lord, from the depths of the pit; Thou didst hear my plea, "Do not close Thine ear to my cry for help!" Thou didst come near when I called on Thee; Thou didst say, "Do not fear!"' (Lamentations 3:55-57).

## ii. Elijah

Another prophet, Elijah, is remembered for his enormous stature, bravery and faithfulness. When all seemed apostate, he did not and would not budge or bend. A more prayerful and faithful man of God we could not meet. Elijah is perhaps best known for his victorious exploits on Mount Carmel as recorded in 1 Kings 18. How Elijah showed up idolatry! How he glorified the true God! Oh to be like Elijah...! and yet, 'Elijah was a man of like nature with ourselves' (James 5:17), for just one chapter later, in 1 Kings 19, we see that Elijah went from a peak to a trough. The very same man who was so successful and victorious said 'It is enough, now O Lord, take away my life ...' (1 Kings 19:4). The remedy God prescribed for his depressed condition was food and sleep. This remedy is not exactly 'spiritual', but it does remind us how our physical state can effect our mental and spiritual well being. Depression can have a physical cause. Even today a good night's sleep or a week away from it all can be most effective in lifting the clouds and renewing our perspective and outlook.

## iii. John the Baptist

According to Jesus, John the Baptist was the greatest man who ever lived. 'Truly, I say to you, among those born of woman there has risen no one greater than John the Baptist' (Matthew 11:11). And yet this greatest of men suffered a severe shake of faith. When locked in a prison cell, John was gripped by dark doubts, and asked of the Jesus he had formerly proclaimed 'Are you He Who is to come, or shall we look for another?' (Matthew 11:3). It is an obvious point but worth mentioning that circumstances and the stranger providences can affect our inner state and even throw us off-centre at times.

The Bible then is most realistic. It is well aware of the phenomenon of depression. If John the Baptist had a 'down', how much more likely are we. To be forewarned is to be forearmed. The *Westminster Confession* reminds us:-

> '... faith... may be often and many ways assailed and weakened ... ' and also 'true believers may have the assurance of their salvation divers ways shaken, diminished and intermitted ... by some sudden or vehement temptation, by God's withdrawing the light of His countenance and suffering even such as fear Him to walk in darkness and to have no light... yet... by the operation of the Spirit, this assurance may, in due time, be revived; and by the which, in the mean time, they are supported from utter despair.'

Both the Bible and our Confessions then realise that there is a darker side to life. Be warned: 'the days of darkness will be many' (Ecclesiastes 11:8).

## 2. THE BIBLE REGARDS THE DARKNESS OF DEPRESSION

If we open the Bible, almost at random, we cannot fail to see but one thing, and that is that God cares. God cares! He knows us through and through, 'inside out and back to front' and is better acquainted with our physical and psychological condition than we are or ever will be. 'He cares about you' (1 Peter 5:7). 'As a father pities his children, so the Lord pities those who fear Him. For He knows our frame; He remembers that we are dust' (Psalm 103:13,14). Our Maker knows our physical and psychological frame most intimately. 'Even the hairs of your head are all numbered' (Luke 12:7).

If we ever doubt that God cares, consider that in Jesus Christ, God cared enough to become Man to save us from our sins. Christ's death on the cross delivers all who believe in Him from eternal hell - a place and state infinitely worse than even the darkest depression.

Even a cursory reading of the Gospels shows that much of Jesus's earthly ministry was spent ministering to troubled souls and mending broken lives - and He has not changed one iota. 'Jesus Christ is the same yesterday and today and forever' (Hebrews 13:8). He is the heavenly Physician Who understands all our visible and invisible ills. 'Those who are well have no need of a physician' (Mark 2:17). We often read this statement concerning the Lord Jesus Christ's ministry here on earth: 'He had compassion' (Matthew 9:36, Matthew 14:14, Luke 7:13 et al). This word 'compassion' is a strong one. It shows how Jesus was inwardly moved and filled with practical pity whenever He came across human need and suffering - and He is still the same!

Jesus disturbed the comfortable, for sure, but He also comforted the disturbed. Jesus broke hard hearts and yet He also healed broken hearts. His mandate was predicted as far back as Isaiah 61:1 'He has sent Me to bind up the brokenhearted' – and Jesus is still the same! This being so, we can take our earthly depression to our Heavenly Physician, and pour out our hearts to Him. We need never feel ashamed or afraid in His tender company. The best of our friends here below might dismiss us with a "Pull yourself together!" but not so the Lord Jesus. The Bible is absolutely and unequivocally clear about His infinite sensitivity and tenderness. 'He will not break a bruised reed or quench a smouldering wick' (Matthew 12:20). What a Friend we have in Jesus!

*Have we trials and temptations?*
*Is there trouble anywhere?*
*We should never be discouraged*
*Take it to the Lord in prayer!*
*Can we find a Friend so faithful*
*Who will all our sorrows share?*
*Jesus knows our every weakness*
*Take it to the Lord in prayer.*

Finally, consider that:-

## 3. THE BIBLE REFORMS THE DARKNESS OF DEPRESSION

None of us will ever enjoy depression, as it seems to sap all our inner vitality, causing us to live in slow motion - 'a downcast spirit dries up the bones' (Proverbs 17:22). Unlikely as it sounds however, good can result from it. The Bible assures us 'that in everything God works for good with those who love Him' (Romans 8:28) - and the Bible here does not have an 'exception clause' reading 'in everything but depression.' There is nothing that the Lord cannot sanctify to us, and use to our greater good and His glory - even depression. At the very least, if we have been in the pit of a depressed despair, we will be much more understanding and sympathetic, less harsh and less quick to judge, and better able to help and stand alongside others. Those who have never yet experienced depression are totally oblivious to and unaware of its blackness, and could never fathom its seeming hopelessness. Depression is worse than physical sickness. Physical sickness is unsubtle. 'A man's spirit will endure sickness; but a broken spirit who can bear?' (Proverbs 18:14).

But can depression, a diss-ease of the spirit aid us spiritually? I believe that it can. Follow closely while I explain:-

The busy-ness of life in the late 20th century can get so great that our relationship with God suffers, being crowded out by lesser matters, (c.f. Luke 10:40 'Martha was distracted with much serving'). Depression however can free us from the noise, hurryings, confusion and feverish clamour of life and give us that totally empty and solitary feeling - almost a complete and infinite inner void. It is at times like these that we can experience the presence and closeness of God in a very special way, when all temporal props have been taken away, and the feverish pace of life has been stilled. God fills the infinite void in our hearts with His love. He really does. Scripture affirms that this is so:–

'God opposes the proud but gives grace to the humble' (1 Peter 5:5).

'The sacrifice acceptable to God is a broken spirit; a broken and contrite heart, O God, Thou wilt not despise' (Psalm 51:17), and especially 'The Lord is near to the broken hearted, and saves the crushed in spirit' (Psalm 34:18).

Depression, you see, brings us into the 'Valley of Humiliation' - and in this valley we meet God. 'Great-Heart,' the archetypal Christian Pastor in *Pilgrim's Progress* tells us more about the blessings to be found in this Valley:-

> In this valley our Lord formerly had His country home; He loved much to be here. He loved also to walk these meadows, for He found the air pleasant. Besides, here a man shall be free from the noise and from the hurryings of this life. All states are full of noise and confusion; only the Valley of Humiliation is that empty and solitary place. Here a man shall not be so let and hindered in his contemplation as in other places he is apt to be. This is a valley that nobody walks in but those that love a pilgrim's life ... in former times men met with angels here, have found pearls here, and have in this place found the words of life.
>
> Did I say our Lord had here in former days His country house and that He loved here to walk? I will add, in this place, and to the people that live and trace these grounds, He has left a yearly revenue to be faithfully paid them at certain seasons for their maintenance by the way and for their further encouragement to go on in their pilgrimage.

The Bible then certainly does help those who are depressed, offering the comfort of none less than Almighty God to those in its slough. It realises that depression exists, it promises the help and grace of God to those who suffer from such, and it assures us that good can ensue from it.

In closing, remember that on the cross, Jesus tasted the absolute depths. The very skies were darkened and God the Father forsook Him as He bore God's wrath to pardon our sins. Hell is eternal separation from the love and light of God, and on the cross, Jesus tasted that eternal desolation in a moment of time, so that all who believe in Him may be saved from eternal depression, and enjoy God's eternal life and joy. The Gospel then is the ultimate answer. Let us therefore seek to walk by faith and not by sight, and strive to believe the Bible when it assures us that, if we belong to Jesus, no matter how low our mood may be, now or in the future, 'neither height nor depth nor anything else in all creation will be able to separate us from the love of God in Christ Jesus our Lord' (Romans 8:39).

*O child of God, wait patiently*
*When dark the path may be*
*And let thy faith lean trustingly*
*On Him Who cares for thee*
*And though the clouds hang drearily*
*Upon the brow of night*
*Yet in the morning joy will come*
*And fill thy soul with light.*

# Biblical Comfort For The Lonely

*I will not leave you desolate, I will come to you*
*(John 14:18).*

## 1. THE PRESENCE OF GOD WITHIN US

'I will not leave you desolate, I will come to you' (John 14:18), promised the Saviour to His frightened disciples, when they were filled with sadness by the news that the dearest Friend they had ever known was about to leave them. 'I will not leave you desolate' He promised to them and promises to us. The word 'desolate' here is the word 'orphanos' – orphans. One is reminded of Psalm 27:10 'For my Father and my mother have forsaken me, but the Lord will take me up.'

But we may wonder whether we really can enjoy the presence of Jesus with us, healing our loneliness, as when He was here on earth, He could only minister to one person at one time. A few verses earlier we are assured that we really can, for Jesus promises the personal presence of the Holy Spirit to all those who believe in Him. 'I will pray the Father and He will give you another Counsellor, to be with you forever, even the Spirit of truth, Whom the world cannot receive, because it neither sees Him nor knows Him; you know Him for He dwells with you and will be in you' (John 14:16, 17).

The Holy Spirit is the third Person of the Trinity. He is named as the 'Parakletos' in the original. A Parakletos means 'one called alongside to help,' 'Comforter,' 'Ally, friend,' 'Strengthener, encourager.' In 1 John 2:1 Jesus Himself is termed 'Parakletos.' It follows then that enjoying the presence of the Holy Spirit - 'another Parakletos' - is the same, experientially, as enjoying the wonderful presence of Jesus Himself - the only difference being that now many more people can enjoy this wonderful presence than they did in first century Palestine. The Holy Spirit may be thought of as the true 'Vicar of Christ on earth.' We can see then why Jesus was to say a little later 'I tell you the truth: it is to your advantage that I go away, for if I do not go away, the Counsellor will not come to you' (John 16:7).

The blessed Holy Spirit of God within us and around us is God's super-abundantly sufficient solution for human loneliness. If God condescended to become man and live in a human body at the first Christmas (which He did), how much more does He condescend today, when, by His Holy Spirit, He takes up residence in human hearts, making the transcendent God imminent. ' . . . we will come and make our home with him' (John 14:23). 'Do you not know that your body is a temple of the Holy Spirit within you, which you have from God?' (1 Corinthians 6:18).

> *Our blest Redeemer, ere He breathed*
> *His tender last farewell,*
> *A guide, a comforter bequeathed*
> *With us to dwell.*

Rev. Donald M. Macleod in his booklet *The Doctrine of the Holy Spirit* comments most helpfully:-

> When the Saviour left this world, He promised that He would give another Comforter to His Own... He was to sustain and comfort the disciples in their sorrow, and He was to abide with the Church for ever, His work being to support, cherish, relieve and comfort her in all her tribulations. In this we see infinite condescension - God humbling Himself

to behold things on the earth and to discharge such an office on behalf of poor worms of dust. We also see His wondrous love - that love which passeth knowledge and which is spread abroad in the heart by the Holy Ghost.

'God... gives His Holy Spirit to you' (1 Thessalonians 4:8). 'God's love has been poured into our hearts through the Holy Spirit which has been given to us' (Romans 5:5). Thank God for His Holy Spirit. Enjoying His presence within us is the Divine provision for loneliness – as also are:-

## 2. THE PEOPLE OF GOD AROUND US

In his published lectures entitled *Christian Doctrine*, J.S. Whale has a chapter entitled 'Life in the Spirit.' Here he makes the comment:- 'The thought of the New Testament about redemption is as much corporate and communal, as it is individual and personal. This two-fold truth is the key to the Christian doctrine of the Church.'

Of course, the Christian Faith is an intensely personal matter; it begins when we trust Christ as our own, personal Saviour and receive and appropriate all the benefits of His finished Calvary Work for ourself. No one else can believe for us. We cannot be saved by proxy. This being so, however, salvation does not finish there, for by believing in Christ we are united to the body of Christ and so become a member of His Church - the Church which, according to the New Testament, is 'the body of Christ,' (see Ephesians 1:22,23). In a body there is never an isolated independence of the individual members, only a corporate inter-dependence - and it is the same in the body of Christ. 'For just as the body is one and has many members, and all the members of the body, though many, are one body, so it is with Christ... Now you are the body of Christ and individually members of it' (1 Corinthians 12:12,27). The New Testament knows nothing of an isolated Christian. All Christians are members of the body of Christ, and should be and need to be enjoying the company and fellowship of other believers in the community of the redeemed.

## The Church

In 1 Timothy 3:15 and Ephesians 2:19, the Church is described as 'the household of God.' Similarly, Galatians 6:10 mentions 'the household of faith.' The Church then is God's family - and we saw in an earlier chapter that when we are born again, God adopts us into this family, a family transcending both the world and the ages. Being in God's family is God's provision for human loneliness. In a different context, God Himself said 'It is not good that the man should be alone . . .' (Genesis 2:18), and the principle may be applied in relation to the Christian and the Church. In Christ, God reconciles us both to Himself and to one another. It is Christ Who breaks our unhappy barriers and divisions down, bringing our sinful, self-centred isolation and suspicion to an end. 'There is neither Jew nor Greek, there is neither slave nor free, there is neither male nor female, for you are all one in Christ Jesus' (Galatians 3:28).

How we need the Church! We cannot survive without the spiritual sustenance which she provides, or without the mutual help and support of our fellow believers. The exhortation is still most relevant to every Christian 'let us consider how to stir up one another to love and good works, not neglecting to meet together, as is the habit of some, but encouraging one another ...' (Hebrews 10:23,24). If a personal testimony may be allowed, I can honestly say that wherever I have lived I have been well taken care of by God's people. The Lord has always provided me with a Bible-believing church whose ministry has been a blessing; the Lord has always provided me with the most wonderful of Christian people who have welcomed me into their hearts and homes, treating me as a member of their family - which, of course, spiritually speaking, I am. In Christ, God is our Father, and fellow believers are our brothers and sisters. Truly, 'God gives the desolate a home to dwell in' (Psalm 68:6).

A word which encapsulates the communal life of the redeemed is the word 'Fellowship.' Fellowship expresses the idea of 'sharing, partnership, having something in common or sharing a common way of life.' The Christian Faith is all about fellowship with God and fellowship with God's people, both in this life and the next. John explained that the purpose of his first letter was 'so that you may have fellowship with us; and our fellowship is with the Father and with His Son Jesus Christ' (1 John 1:3). Let us allow Professor J.I.Packer's expertise to have the last word on this:-

Fellowship with God ... is the source from which fellowship among Christians springs; and fellowship with God is the end to which Christian fellowship is a means. We should not, therefore, think of our fellowship with other Christians as a spiritual luxury, an optional addition to the exercises of private devotion. We should recognise rather that such fellowship is a spiritual necessity; for God has made us in such a way that our fellowship with Himself is fed by our fellowship with fellow-Christians, and requires to be so fed constantly for its own deepening and enrichment.

*Blest be the tie that binds*
*Our hearts in Christian love*
*The fellowship of kindred minds*
*Is like to that above*

*We share our mutual woes*
*Our mutual burdens bear*
*And often for each other flows*
*The sympathetic tear.*

Thank God for His Church! It is His answer to human loneliness. But loneliness will not however be fully and finally eradicated until we enter:-

## 3. THE PARADISE OF GOD ABOVE US

Whilst all that we have said so far is, and can be, gloriously true, life in the Spirit here on earth is but a foretaste of the glorious life awaiting the believer in heaven. We may enjoy God's presence now - but we will enjoy it perfectly then. We may fellowship with God's people now, but our fellowship will be much greater and fuller then, for then it will be unhindered and unmarred by the sin which will indwell even the redeemed until their dying day. (Even the best church families have their squabbles!)

God's ultimate answer to loneliness is heaven – 'Paradise restored' (see the author's *My Father's House*.) The Spirit of God within us is just a foretaste of the greater glory to come. Every Christian is 'sealed with the promised Holy Spirit, which is a guarantee of our inheritance until we acquire possession of it, to the praise of His glory' (Ephesians 1:13,14).

For the Christian, heaven is home. 'Home' is such a lovely word. It conjures up images of people and places we love and with whom we feel at ease. This being so, Philippians 1:23 speaks for itself and for us all:- 'My desire is to depart and be with Christ, for that is far better.'

As heaven is our ultimate home, is it surprising if we do feel some twinges of homesickness and loneliness here on earth? We are a long way from home!

*O sweet and blessed country*
*The home of God's elect*
*O sweet and blessed country*
*That eager hearts expect...*

Lonely Christian then take heart! Your loneliness is not forever. Jesus is preparing a place for you in heaven right now. He says to you:- 'Let not your hearts be troubled; believe in God, believe also in Me. In My Father's house are many rooms; if it were not so, would I have told you that I go to prepare a place for you?' (John 14:1,2).

## CONCLUSION

The main thesis of this book is that Jesus Christ is the ultimate answer to the deepest human needs - and this is definitely the case here. Jesus Christ is the answer to loneliness. His death on the cross for our sins is the only way to restore us to harmony with God. His Spirit within us enables us to enjoy His companionship through all the ups and downs of our earthly life. His provision of the Church, the fellowship of believing brothers and sisters, will supply all the needed help and support as we travel heavenwards, and in heaven, the bliss, glory and total harmony will abundantly compensate us for everything that we perceive we have missed out upon here on earth.

## A Warning

If however, you are not a Christian, as tenderly as I can, I say that it is no wonder that you are lonely. You are lonely because you are separated from God your Maker – the source of all love, life, light and comfort. Worst of all, if you should continue to be outside of Jesus Christ, you are heading for eternal loneliness in outer darkness, away from the love and light of God. This lonely, outer darkness of hell is the eternal 'home' of all who are outside of Christ, having rejected God's mercy in Him. This being so, 'we beseech you on behalf of Christ, be reconciled to God' (2 Corinthians 5:20) by trusting in the crucified Christ to save you. It is Jesus Christ alone who gives us the comforting assurance that our eternal home will be heaven – the glorious and harmonious city of the New Jerusalem, characterised by unblemished fellowship with God and one another.

> *Where will you spend Eternity -*
> *Those years that have no end?*
> *Will it be on the golden shore*
> *Safe with the friends that have gone before*
> *Safe and happy for evermore?*
>
> *Eternity, Eternity -*
> *Where will you spend Eternity?*

# Four Cheers For You

*Be of good cheer!...*
(Matthew 9:2,14:27, John 16:33, Acts 23:11, AV)

## GOSPEL CHEER

We may take it as a self evident biblical truth that the Gospel is the only true and lasting comfort and cheer that we have. The Gospel brings an inner cheer that the world just cannot give, and thankfully, the world cannot take away. 'The kingdom of God is ... righteousness, peace and *joy* in the Holy Spirit' (Romans 14:17). 'God our Father ... loved us and gave us eternal comfort and good hope through grace' (2 Thessalonians 2:16).

The Gospel is God's Own gift of hope and cheer for this dark and dismal world, and in this chapter, I would like us to focus on not three, but 'four cheers' of the Bible, literally 'four cheers' to cheer our hearts. I shall be using the King James Version which translates each one as 'Be of good cheer!' - other versions say the same thing but differently, using expressions such as 'Take heart!' or 'Be of good courage!' We will do well to hide these 'cheers' in our hearts and make them our own.

## 1. THE CHEER OF HIS PARDON

In Matthew 9:2, Jesus says 'Son, BE OF GOOD CHEER; Thy sins be forgiven thee.' These certainly were cheerful words to the one originally addressed, for the one originally addressed was a paralysed man, totally dependent on other peoples' good-will for his mobility and well-being. But no sooner had Jesus spoken these words of pardoning cheer than he was healed! Leaping up to new life he folded up the mat on which he lay, and went joyfully on his way home. He certainly would never forget the day Jesus said to him 'Be of good cheer!' How ever could he?

We too can enjoy (except in a spiritual sense) exactly the same cheer as that un-named paralysed man, if we have heard Jesus's word of pardon to our souls. Divine forgiveness is so liberating. Divine forgiveness is only possible because Jesus died on the cross for our sins, shedding His very life blood for our pardon. If we have experienced the pardoning power of the blood of Christ, we may be assured that all is ultimately well with our souls. His blood is our eternal life assurance – and what joy this divine quality of life brings. 'Be of good cheer, thy sins be forgiven thee.' 'Who can forgive sins but God alone?...' (Matthew 9:2, Mark 2:7). It was a pertinent question. The whole incident of the healing of the paralytic shows that Jesus Christ is God. His pardon brings Divine cheer for our dismal, damned human hearts – just as it did to the paralytic's. This then is our first cheer. The cheer of His pardon.

> *Oh sing of my redeemer*
> *His praise my theme shall be*
> *He took my sins upon Him*
> *And bore them on the tree*

## 2. THE CHEER OF HIS PEACE

'*. . .the ship was now in the midst of the sea, tossed with waves ... they cried out for fear. But straightway Jesus spoke unto them "BE OF GOOD CHEER; it is I; be not afraid"*' (Matthew 14:24,27).

These words 'Be of good cheer', when spoken in their original context to Jesus's disciples were desperately welcome. Put yourself in the disciples' position on that occasion. There they were, out alone, sailing on the Sea of

Galilee. It was the middle of the night and the most fearful storm had erupted. How frightened they were - even though some of them were experienced sailors. Jesus came just when they needed Him therefore, speaking this genuinely 'cheer-ful' word of peace. 'Be of good cheer; it is I; be not afraid.' How cheerful and relieving is the peace Jesus imparts.

We have no difficulty in relating to those disciples when they felt so threatened and almost engulfed by the waves. The 'storms of life' can make us feel so weak and vulnerable in our 'little boats'. Jesus's words to us in our stormy situations are very reassuring: 'Be of good cheer, it is I, be not afraid.' It is so good to know that Jesus stands by us through all the storms of life. Jesus gives us peace amidst our storms; and also, if He so chooses (being the omnipotent Lord of all) He can deliver us from all our storms, calming the most troubled of waters. 'Be not afraid', He says to us today.

I have a booklet called *Fascinating Facts About The Bible*. One of the 'fascinating facts' it gives is this:- 'The two words 'Fear not' are said to be repeated seventy four times in the Bible.' I once heard a preacher go further. He said that the words 'Fear not' and similar, such as 'Be not afraid' actually occur three hundred and sixty six times in the Bible. Assuming he was right, we have a 'Fear not' for every day of the year including a leap year.

The cheer of Jesus's peace is a priceless commodity. He is the 'Prince of Peace' (Isaiah 9:6). He gives us 'peace with God' (Romans 5:1). He imparts 'the peace of God which passes understanding' (Philippians 4:7). Listen to what He said: 'Peace I leave with you, My peace I give to you; not as the world gives do I give to you. Let not your hearts be troubled, neither let them be afraid' (John 14:27). This reminds us of a lovely verse in the Old Testament: 'Thou wilt keep Him in perfect peace, whose mind is stayed on Thee, because he trusts in Thee' (Isaiah 26:3). Fear and peace are diametrically opposed. The antidote to fear is to drown ourselves in the love of God, for His 'perfect love casts out fear' (1 John 4:18). Here then is the cheer of Jesus's peace. ... 'making peace by the blood of His cross' (Colossians 1:20).

*Peace, perfect peace, in this dark world of sin?*
*The blood of Jesus whispers peace within.*

## 3. THE CHEER OF HIS POWER

In John 16:33, shortly before His cruel and ignominious death, Jesus said these remarkable words to His disciples: 'In the world ye shall have tribulation: but BE OF GOOD CHEER; I have overcome the world.'

We all know what tribulation is. Trials and tribulations, 'losses and crosses' are intricately woven by God into our Christian pilgrimage. 'Through many tribulations we must enter the kingdom of God' (Acts 14:22). It is both cheering and encouraging to know that Jesus is greater than all our tribulations. By His death and resurrection, Jesus overcame the world and its evil - and He shares this all-powerful conquest with us as 'we are more than conquerors through Him Who loved us' (Romans 8:37). 'Who shall separate us from the love of Christ?... shall tribulation?' (Romans 8:35). 'Who is it that overcomes the world but he who believes that Jesus is the Son of God?' (1 John 5:5). 'Thanks be to God Who gives us the victory through our Lord Jesus Christ' (1 Corinthians 15:57).

Whatever our circumstances therefore, God has given us the resources to be cheerful. If we walk by sight we will be fearful – it would seem as though evil was winning. But if we walk by faith we will remember that King Jesus reigns. (cf 2 Corinthians 5:6,7: 'So we are always of good courage . . . for we walk by faith, not by sight . . .'). Satan is powerful, but Jesus is all-powerful. His final words on earth were 'All authority on heaven and earth has been given to Me' (Matthew 28:18). Be of good cheer! For our fourth and final 'cheer', let us consider:-

## 4. THE CHEER OF HIS PRESENCE

'A word in season, how good it is!' (Proverbs 15:23), and genuine words of cheer are always in season. Such a word was given by Jesus to the Apostle Paul at a crucial stage in Paul's life. At the time Paul's immediate future was most uncertain. He had so many enemies and was yet again in prison for the Gospel. Luke relates that it was at this critical moment when 'the Lord stood by him (Paul) and said "BE OF GOOD CHEER, Paul ..."' (Acts 23:11). Here we see the cheer of His presence – the wonderful presence of Jesus. Truly, 'there is a friend who sticks closer than a brother' (Proverbs 18:24).

If we are Christ's, we can take heart that, no matter how fearful and intimidating our external conditions may be, He will stand with us and by us right to the end. His presence makes all the difference. His closing words on earth were 'lo, I am with you always, to the close of the age' (Matthew 28:20), and God assures us in the Bible "I will never fail you nor forsake you." Hence we can confidently say, "The Lord is my helper, I will not be afraid; what can man do to me?" (Hebrews 13:5,6). What a Friend we have in Jesus. He is a Friend for life, a Friend in Death, and, praise His name, a Friend for all eternity.

## CONCLUSION

So here are four 'cheers' for us in this fallen world which, at times, can seem so gloomy and cheer-less. We cannot really expect unalloyed joy in this life, for the highest earthly joys are so very fragile, and sin, the ultimate cause of misery will not be fully and finally eradicated until the Lord inaugurates the new heavens and the new earth. This apart though, Jesus commands us to 'BE OF GOOD CHEER'. Even in this life we may know something of the 'cheer of the Lord' and rejoice in the pardon, peace, power and presence of Jesus. This 'divine cheer' really does make an eternity of difference.

*Who can cheer the heart like Jesus, By His presence all Divine?*
*True and tender, pure and precious, O how blest to call Him mine!*
*All that thrills my soul is Jesus; He is more than life to me;*
*And the fairest of ten thousand, in my blessed Lord I see.*

# $\mathcal{M}$y Times Are In God's Hand

*My times are in Thy hand*
**(Psalm 31:15).**

There is enormous comfort and solace to be gained from being able to look up to God, irrespective of our circumstances, and confess 'My times are in Thy hand' (Psalm 31:15). By this we mean that *all* of our times are in God's hands, bad days as well as good, sad days as well as joyful, the boring days, the frustrating days, the devastating days... all of them. Biblically, there is no such thing as 'a chance event' or 'fate.' 'The lot is cast into the lap, but the decision is wholly from the Lord' (Proverbs 16:33).

From the perspective of the Bible, even the minutest details of our lives have all been foreordained by God. Jesus explained this by contrasting an insignificant sparrow with one of His followers:- 'Are not two sparrows sold for a penny? And not one of them will fall to the ground without your Father's will. But even the hairs of your head are all numbered. Fear not therefore; you are of more value than many sparrows' (Matthew 10:29-30). Do we really believe Jesus here? Hard providences will soon reveal whether we believe in the heart as well as in the head. The subject of 'Trials' makes an interesting topic for Bible topic debates, but when they arrive on our own agenda, with the pain and bewilderment they often bring, we learn to view them more as the Lord intends. It is in the cauldron of suffering that our faith is tested as to whether we really do 'know that in everything God works for good with those who love Him, who are called according to His purpose' (Romans 8:28).

The comfort of being able to say 'My times are in Thy hand' from the heart just cannot be measured. It gives the assurance that "God is in control of my life" when times verge on the unbearable. God is in control - not 'chance' or 'fate' and certainly not the Devil. It is thus as inconceivable that our lives could get out of His good and wise control as it is that the world could spin off its axis. Suffering Job knew this. Amidst intense anguish and pain, he yet confessed 'But He knows the way that I take; when He has tried me, I shall come forth as gold' (Job 23:10).

There are two truths of the Bible that we would do well to take to heart and, make a part of our very fibre. 1. God is sovereign 2. God is good. The Scriptural proof for these axioms include:– 1. 'The Lord has established His throne in the heavens, and His kingdom rules over all' (Psalm 103:19) 2. 'This God - His way is perfect' (Psalm 18:31). This being so, 'theo-logical' logic reasons: 1. Nothing can ever happen to me unless God has ordained it - His sovereignty ensures that 2. Nothing can ever happen to me which is not for my ultimate good - His goodness ensures that. We can see now how David, in our Psalm, moved from saying 'I have passed out of mind like one who is dead; I have become a broken vessel' (Psalm 31:12) to 'But I trust in Thee O Lord, I say "Thou art my God." My times are in Thy hand' (Psalm 31:14,15) to ending the Psalm with the happy exhortation 'Be strong and let your heart take courage, all you who wait for the Lord' (Psalm 31:24). David here passed from madness to courage, all from knowing 'My times are in Thy hand.' Possessing this outlook on life – or rather being possessed by such an outlook – is both stabilizing and comforting. 'For from Him and through Him and to Him are all things' (Romans 11:36).

*Every joy or trial*
*Falleth from above*
*Traced upon life's dial*
*By the Sun of love*
*We may trust Him fully*
*All for us to do*
*They who trust Him wholly*
*Find Him wholly true.*

## PROVIDENCE

A way of crystallising the truth of 'My times are in Thy hand' is to consider both God's eternal decree and His comforting providence. These are technical terms, but easily understood. Of the former, the *Westminster Confession of Faith* states:-

'God, from all eternity, did, by the most wise and holy counsel of His Own will, freely and unchangeably ordain whatsoever comes to pass...' (chapter 3). And of the latter, it teaches:-

'God the great Creator of all things doth uphold, direct, dispose and govern all creatures, actions, and things, from the greatest even to the least, by His most wise and holy providence ...'(Chapter 5).

Confessing that 'My times are in Thy hand' is to transfer 'Providence' from a merely theoretical concept to a personal and practical reality. To strengthen our belief that all the minutie of our lives really are taken care of by God, let us now explore the theme further.

## PROVIDENCE EXPOUNDED

According to the Bible, God knew all about us even before we were born. He said to young Jeremiah at the beginning of his ministry: 'Before I formed you in the womb I knew you' (Jeremiah 1:5). The Psalmist expounds this further, confessing to God 'Thou didst form my inward parts, Thou didst knit me together in my mother's womb ... Thou knowest me right well; my frame was not hidden from Thee, when I was made in secret, intricately wrought in the depths of the earth. Thy eyes beheld my unformed substance; in Thy book were written, every one of them, the days that were yet formed for me, when as yet there was none of them' (Psalm 139:15,16).

When we analyse it, why were we born at all? Did we give God our permission to come into this world at the exact moment that we did? Of course not! It was all totally out of our control. 'As you do not know how the spirit comes to the bones in the womb of a woman with child, so you do not know the work of God Who makes everything' (Ecclesiastes 11:5). Knowledge of this fact alone can deepen our dependance on and trust in God. How helpless we really are. We had no say at all over our birth - God had it all. There is a gentle rebuke for us here. 'Woe to Him who strives with his Maker, an earthen vessel with the potter! Does the clay say to Him who fashions it, 'What are you making?' or 'Your work has no handles'? Woe to him who says to a Father 'What are you begetting?' or to a woman 'With what are you in travail?' Thus says the Lord, the Holy One of Israel and His Maker: 'Will you question Me about my children, or command Me concerning the work of My hands?...'" (Isaiah 45:9-11).

Not only is our birth in God's hands, but, at the other end of the spectrum, the exact moment and day of our death too is totally in His hands. Paul proclaimed this to the Athenians. God has, Paul said 'determined allotted periods' (Acts 17:26), that is, God has determined exactly how long our hearts will beat upon this earth. 'In Thy book were written, everyone of them, the days that were formed for me, when as yet there were none of them' (Psalm 139:16). What a comfort this is. We can consider our deaths to be a date already written down in God's diary, and we are immortal until God calls us home. We will not die a moment before God's time – just as we will not live a moment longer than He sees fit. Our lives are in His hands and our deaths are in His hands likewise - whether He sees fit to terminate our lives by old age, illness, 'accident' or even a terrorist's bullet. In being gripped by this thought, the Psalmist was led to exclaim 'How precious to me are Thy thoughts O God' (Psalm 139:17). We can no more leave this world prematurely, than we can bring ourselves into this world before our time.

> *Death and plagues around me fly*
> *Till He bid, I cannot die*
> *Not a single shaft can hit*
> *Till the love of God sees fit.*

The Bible also teaches that God has determined the 'where' of our life as well as its 'when.' Why do we live where we do? Because God has placed us here, 'having determined allotted periods and the boundaries of their habitation' (Acts 17:26). We had no choice in the matter of being born in the rich and prosperous west, as opposed to being born into the poverty and squalor of the third world. This is cause for humble thanksgiving. In another Psalm,

David exclaimed 'Thou holdest my lot. The lines have fallen for me in pleasant places; yea, I have a goodly heritage' (Psalm 16:6). And what a heritage! Consider the plight of one being born into a militant Islamic state for instance. How good of God to put us into a land where the Gospel is preached. How good of God to put us into a land of the open Bible, with freedom of evangelism and where Christians can meet together for worship and fellowship without any fear of persecution.

## GOD'S PROVIDENTIAL SALVATION

Think back to the time when you first entered into the joy of God's salvation. It may be that you cannot recall the exact time and date, but whenever it was, you know that you now belong to Jesus, having trusted in Him and His death on the cross for full pardon of your sins and peace with God. Well, in spite of what people say about 'free-will,' we had as little power over our supernatural, spiritual re-birth as we did over our natural, physical birth. The new birth is all the sovereign work of God the Father, Son and Holy Spirit. 'You, He made alive, when you were dead through the trespasses and sins in which you once walked' (Ephesians 2:1). It is God Who gives us spiritual life as well as physical life. In this He is totally sovereign, bestowing it upon some whilst witholding it from others. We read in the Bible, for instance, of a lady by the name of Lydia. Lydia was converted to Christ through Paul's preaching. Lydia was thus born again, but notice carefully that 'The Lord opened her heart to give heed to what was said to her by Paul' (Acts 16:14). Thank God that our salvation too is not by chance or a 'hit and miss' affair. Never! 'He chose us in Him before the foundation of the world' (Ephesians 1:4). Those whom God has chosen in Christ in eternity past, will, in time, come to to trust in Him for full salvation. God's eternal decree and irresistible grace and effectual calling make it all so certain. Thank God for His effectual calling. 'Effectual calling is the work of God's Spirit, whereby, convincing us of our sin and misery, enlightening our minds in the knowledge of Christ and renewing our wills, He doth persuade and enable us to embrace Jesus Christ, freely offered to us in the Gospel.' (*Shorter Catechism*, Q.31). The God Who ordained the end of salvation ordained the means to salvation as well - be it a Christian family, tract, book, preacher or teacher, or whoever or however He sees fit to bring the good news of salvation.

Stop for a moment and trace the events which led to your being saved. Humanly speaking, how complex it all was. There were no doubt so many seemingly insurmountable barriers to our ever coming to personal faith in Christ. But God raised us from the dead! He softened our hard hearts, He opened our blind eyes and He unstopped our deaf ears so that we are now alive in Christ. We are – but others are not. Our times are in His hands. 'Those whom He predestined He also called; and those whom He called He also justified; and those whom He justified He also glorified' (Romans 8:30). In the sight of the eternal God and great I AM, predestination and glorification are all one.

## THE PAINFUL PROVIDENCES

Coming somewhat down to earth however, what of the hurtful and even wicked things that have come our way? It is here that 'the rubber grips the road.' For example, Where was God when my mother developed Altzeimer's Disease? Where was God when my child was killed by a drunken driver? Where is God when I apply and apply for jobs but keep on getting the same old morale-breaking rejection slips that seem so interminable? To answer such questions we must tread most tenderly, carefully and above all Biblically. The Bible does not give us any glib, pat answers to the mystery of suffering. It rather encourages us to trust God even when it hurts and when we cannot understand. Warren Wiersbe sometimes says 'We live by God's promises, not God's explanations.'

Allow me to quote the *Westminster Confession of Faith* once again. Chapter V:iv, attempts some kind of explanation as regards how God's providence and seeming wickedness and sin intersect. It says:-

> The almighty power, unsearchable wisdom and infinite
> goodness of God so far manifest themselves in providence,
> that it extendeth itself even to the first fall and all other sins
> of angels and men; and that not by a bare permission, but

such as hath joined with it a most wise and powerful bound-
ing, and otherwise ordering and governing of them, in a
manifold dispensation, to His own holy ends; yet so, as the
sinfulness thereof proceedeth only from the creature, and
not from God, who, being most holy and righteous, neither
is nor can be the author or approver of sin.

Harsh events, happenings and sufferings are all a fact of our lives. The
touchstone of the maturity of our Christianity, is whether we can still take all
these from the hand of our loving heavenly Father as much as we can the
pleasant and agreeable providences. It has been well said, 'Those who see
the hand of God in everything, will leave everything in the hand of God.'
Romans 11:36 again, 'For from Him and through Him and to Him are all
things.'

There is no reference at all in the Bible any kind of 'dualism,' that is the
notion that good things are from God and bad things are from the Devil.
Biblically, even the Devil is in God's hands, and He uses him for his Own
ends - as He did in the case of Job. God says 'I am the Lord, and there is no
other. I form light and create darkness. I make weal and create woe, I am the
Lord, Who do all these things' (Isaiah 45:7). The Bible even goes as far as
asking the rhetorical question 'Does evil befall a city unless the Lord has
done it?' (Amos 3:6). Lamentations 3:37 and 38 says, amidst almost total devastation 'Who has commanded and it came to pass, unless the Lord has ordained it? Is it not from the mouth of the Most High that good and evil come?'
An awareness of this will lead us to say, even in the most shattering of expe-
riences 'It is the Lord; let Him do what seems good to Him' (1 Samuel 3:18).
Once when I seemed hopelessly unemployed , I stuck this verse on my cup-
board:- 'In the day of prosperity be joyful, and in the day of adversity consider; God has made the one as well as the other' (Ecclesiastes 7:14).

God's ways and wisdom are so much higher than ours (see Isaiah 55:8,9).
We are finite - He is infinite. He is too good to be unkind, and too wise to
make mistakes. Even harsh providences are thus for our ultimate good, even
though their purpose may not be made clear until the next life - 'now I know
in part; then I shall understand fully, even as I have been fully understood'

(1 Corinthians 13:12). There, looking at the completed picture and pattern of our lives, and how all the different pieces fitted so well together, we will not wish anything had been otherwise. Then we will say to God 'O how abundant is Thy goodness, which Thou hast laid up for those who fear Thee, in the sight of the sons of men!' (Psalm 31:19).

## THE MOST WICKED PROVIDENCE OF ALL TIME

Where is God when things seem out of control and we are the recipients of the worst we can imagine? He is right there. To prove it, consider the cross of Christ again. There surely was no more wicked, rebellious and lawless act than the crucifixion of Jesus Christ, when the lovely, harmless, loving, sinless Son of God was taken by cruel men, nailed to a plank of wood and hung up publically to die, as people laughed at Him. God only has one Son, and this was how they treated Him. If wicked men had got the upper hand and 'got one over on' God Himself, frustrating His purpose, surely this was the occasion? But this was far from the case.

It is a mystery and paradox, but in the crucifixion of Christ, even the free and wicked will of men had been foreordained by God for His greater and glorious purposes. 'This Jesus, delivered up according to the definite plan and foreknowledge of God, you crucified and killed by the hands of lawless men' (Acts 2:23). The cross of Jesus therefore, at the very least, gives us some kind of insight into the mystery of how the Divine decree and human wickedness – diametrically opposed though they seem – intersect. In the cross we see how God used wicked men as instruments in bringing about our salvation. He used the absolute worst to bring about the absolute best! Devilish beasts brought about Divine blessing - even though Jesus was the Lamb slain from before the foundation of the world (Revelation 13:8). Therefore, arguing from the greater to the lesser we may state: As God brought about our salvation through the worst tragedy ever, how dare we say He cannot and will not bring blessing through the lesser trials, tribulations and tragedies which we go through. Truly 'He accomplishes all things according to the counsel of His will' (Ephesians 1:11).

'My times are in Thy hand', said King David – and so may we. Living from this Divine perspective changes things. 'He is the God in Whose hand is your breath' (Daniel 5:23). God has foreordained our time in the womb and our time in the tomb, and everything in-between. God foreordained our salvation in Jesus Christ. Nothing can hinder His purposes. The Cross of Christ proves that God has ordained all things that occur in time and space for His glory, and our eternal good.

*My times are in Thy hand*
*My God I wish them there*
*My life my friends my soul I leave*
*Entirely to Thy care*

*My times are in Thy hand*
*Whatever they may be*
*Pleasing or painful, dark or bright*
*As best may seem to Thee*

*My times are in Thy hand*
*Why should I doubt or fear*
*A Father's hand will never cause*
*His child a needless tear*

*My times are in Thy hand*
*Jesus the crucified*
*The hand my cruel sins have grieved*
*Is now my guard and guide*

# Our God Is Human Too

*For we have not a high priest Who is unable to sympathise*
*with our weaknesses, but One Who in every respect*
*has been tempted as we are, yet without sin*
**(Hebrews 4:15).**

## CHRIST'S HUMANITY

It is a tenet of modern liberal theology to cast aspersions on the Deity of Christ, either implicitly or explicitly. Liberal theologians in the past however tended to deny not so much the deity of Christ but rather His real, true and full humanity. The humanity of Christ is actually as equally important as His deity, for if Jesus was not truly human He could not have died for our sins - immortal deity cannot die.

Christ's humanity is a Christian fundamental. The incarnation is central to the Christian Faith. Jesus Christ is the God-man – God in human form. As Christmas comes around each year, Christians throughout the world celebrate the fact that God became man, leaving the glory of heaven, and entering right in to this world of sin and misery. 'God was manifested in the flesh' (1 Timothy 3:16). 'The Word became flesh and dwelt among us . . .' (John 1:14).

The humanity of Christ - the fact that He really did share our human lot - brings home the truth of our text. Our God certainly does know what it is like to be human. He is not a remote God, far removed from human suffering. 'Since ... the children share in flesh and blood, He Himself likewise partook of the same nature' (Hebrews 2:14). It is true then that 'we have not a high priest Who is unable to sympathise with our weaknesses, but one Who in every respect has been tempted as we are, yet without sin' (Hebrews 4:15).

Christ's humanity therefore is more than just an important Christian doctrine. There is great solace and consolation to be gained from knowing that Jesus shared our physical and psychological human frame. This being so, it should prove most helpful if we make a selective catalogue of the humanness of Christ from the Gospel records. In doing so we shall see the true humanity and tender sympathy of the most Sympathetic Friend we can ever know.

## CHRIST'S HUMANITY EXPLORED

Jesus came into this world in the usual way - it was only His conception which was supernatural. We read in the Bible that 'the child grew' (Luke 1:80). His childhood and upbringing were perfectly normal. He experienced all the 'ups and downs' and 'rough and tumble' of normal family life when He grew up in first century Nazareth. Jesus's family was large. It was asked of Him 'Is not this the carpenter, the son of Mary and brother of James and Joses and Judas and Simon, and are not His sisters with us?' (Mark 6:3). Except in the cases of particularly affluent families, first century houses consisted of just one room. Scripture is silent, but we can just imagine the 'give and take' that Jesus had to exercise as He lived at such close quarters, in a family that was far from rich in material terms.

In Jesus, God shared our human lot. He ate (for example, John 21:12), He slept (Mark 4:30), He shared in the joy of a wedding (John 2) and He shared in the grief of a funeral (for example, Luke 7:11-17).

Jesus was no stranger to 'the daily grind.' It was remarked of Him, as we have seen, 'Is this not the carpenter?' (Mark 6:3). He knew what it was like to sweat at His work bench for long hours – and this was before the days of electricity and power tools. Jesus also knew what it was like to experience fatigue. John's Gospel, whilst leaving us in no doubt as regards Jesus's deity, yet records 'Jesus, wearied as He was with His journey, sat down beside the well' (John 4:6).

On a subtler level, Jesus also shared our psychological and emotional lot. The shortest verse in the New Testament reads 'Jesus wept' (John 11:35). The tears that He shed were real. Jesus also knew what it was to be misunderstood, not just by His enemies, but also, even more hurtfully, by those who humanly speaking should have been right behind Him. Scripture records that 'even His brothers did not believe in Him' (John 7:5). And how hurt He must have been when, in a moment of cowardice, Peter, one of His best and closest friends, denied that he even knew Him. Scripture records poignantly 'And the Lord turned and looked at Peter' (Luke 22:61).

Jesus suffered at the hand of peoples' mockery - and psychological humiliation and cruelty can be far harder to take than the less subtle physical persecution. People ironically cast aspersions on the legitimacy of His birth. They taunted Him 'we were not born of fornication; we have one Father, even God' (John 8:41). And then when they hung Him on the cross, stark naked, in severe pain, on a public thoroughfare 'those who passed by derided Him, wagging their heads ... so also the chief priests mocked Him to one another' (Mark 15:29,31) - and all this followed on after His betrayal, unjust trial, scourging, being spat upon and having nails driven through His sinless, sensitive flesh. Being subsequently hung up to die by crucifixion was the ultimate in humiliation, shame and degregation. Old Testament law pronounced 'a hanged man is accursed by God' (Deuteronomy 21:23).

One experience which everyone naturally shrinks from is that of fear. Fear brings a distinctive flavour in the throat and a distinctive flutter in the stomach. All of us have, at some time or other, been wracked by fear - or even total terror - at some impending event. Our fear can be imaginary as well as real, but that does not lessen its unpleasantness. Jesus also knew the terror of impending suffering along with the fear which accompanies it. In the garden of Gethsemene He lay prostrate on the ground as He contemplated the cup of suffering He was about to drink. He knew that this cup entailed Him, the sinless One, actually being 'made sin' (2 Corinthians 5:21), bearing the sins of God's elect in a moment of time, along with God's fearful judgment upon them. It is no wonder then that at that time 'Jesus began to be greatly distressed and troubled' (Mark 14:33). Luke expands a little further telling us:- 'being in an agony He prayed more earnestly; and His sweat became like great drops of blood falling down upon the ground' (Luke 22:44). Maybe it was this that the writer to the Hebrews had in mind when he wrote 'In the days of His flesh, Jesus offered up prayers and supplications, with loud cries and tears, to Him Who was able to save Him from death' (Hebrews 5:7).

I suggested above that many of our fears are ill-founded - they often never materialise; but this was not the case when 'Jesus was greatly distressed and troubled.' His was no imaginary fearful anticipation. On the cross He did actually bear our sin. On the cross He was actually forsaken by God and cried 'My God, my God, why hast Thou forsaken Me?' (Matthew 27:46). The very worst that could happen to anyone - being forsaken by God - actually happened to Jesus, so that the very best that could happen to us - being reconciled to God. The cross teaches us, amongst other things, that Jesus plumbed the very depths of suffering, and no matter what our earthly suffering may be, we can never go any deeper than He has already gone before us when 'by the grace of God He might taste death for every one' (Hebrews 2:9).

## CONCLUSION

When I lived in Belfast, my mother sent me a card, just at the right moment. On it there was a cartoon of a man sitting under a black cloud with the caption JESUS UNDERSTANDS - HE'S BEEN THERE TOO. And so He has! He was a real man, He shared our physiology and psychology, sin apart. What a sympathetic Friend we have in Jesus, Who by His Spirit dwells in us, beside us, underneath us and around us. Truly, 'we have not a high priest Who is unable to sympathise with our weaknesses, but One Who in every respect has been tempted as we are, yet without sin' (Hebrews 4:15). No matter how dark our situation may be therefore, either now or in the future, Jesus really does understand. God knows what it is like to be human – He has been there too.

*No pain that we can share*
*But He has felt its smart*
*All forms of human grief and care*
*Have pierced that tender heart*

*And on His thorn-crowned brow*
*And on His sinless soul*
*Our sins in all their guilt were laid*
*That He might make us whole.*

# God Is Greater Than All Your Troubles

*Mightier than the thunders of many waters, mightier than
the waves of the sea, the Lord on high is mighty*
(Psalm 93:4)

## THE ROYALTY OF THE PSALM

Psalm 93 is a Psalm of confidence. A true reading and inner digestion of its contents will make for confident living - a confidence based, however, not on ourselves, but on God. The Psalm is distinctively God-centred (Theocentric) as opposed to focusing on man.

Psalm 93 begins with God's royal high-ness, and ends with His awesome holiness. The five short verses of the Psalm pack in many of God's attributes, e.g. His Sovereignty (v. 1), His majesty (v.1), His potency (v.1), His eternity (v.2), His omnipotency (v.4), His immutability and purity (v.5) – the whole Psalm being permeated with His greater and absolute glory.

## THE RULING OF THE SOVEREIGN

The opening lines of Psalm 93 reaffirm 'The Lord reigns' (Psalm 93:1). This in itself is most reassuring. A meditation on the total, absolute and all pervading and prevailing sovereignty of God is always a tonic to the soul – doing us especial good when our lives appear to be going out of control. C.H. Spurgeon once said:-

There is no attribute more comforting to His children than God's sovereignty. Under the most adverse circumstances, in the most severe trials, they believe that Sovereignty has ordained their afflictions, that Sovereignty overrules them, and that Sovereignty will sanctify them all. There is nothing for which the children ought more earnestly to contend than the doctrine of their Master over all creation - the Kingship of God over the works of His own hands - the throne of God and His right to sit upon that Throne.

In his commentary on this verse, 'The Lord reigns', Spurgeon reminds us:-

Whatever opposition may arise, His throne is unmoved. He has reigned, does reign and will reign, and will reign for ever and ever. Whatever turmoil and rebellion there may be beneath the clouds, the eternal King sits above all in supreme serenity ... Let us repeat the proclamation 'The Lord reigns', whispering it in the ears of the desponding, and publishing it in the face of the foe ...

'Hallelujah! For the Lord our God the Almighty reigns' (Revelation 19: 6).

*The Lord is King! lift up your voice*
*O earth and all ye heavens, rejoice!*
*From world to world the joy shall ring*
*The Lord omnipotent is King!*

*The Lord is King! who then shall dare*
*Resist His will, distrust His care*
*Or murmur at His wise decrees*
*Or doubt His royal promises?*

## THE RAGING OF THE SEA

Psalm 93, whilst affirming God's total and absolute sovereignty, is nevertheless firmly rooted in reality, well aware of the turmoil of life here on earth. Verse 3 tells us 'The floods have lifted up, O Lord, the floods have lifted up their voice, the floods lift up their roaring.' 'Floods' here may symbolise national, as opposed to personal storms, 'the restless fretfulness of the world against God.' According to the Bible, this world is evil and opposed to God. 'The whole world is in the power of the evil one' (1 John 5:19). The Bible, whilst affirming God's sovereignty also reminds us that the god of this world is the devil - and he has many subjects who render to him their willing obedience. This world then is anti-God. 'Its waters roar and foam ... The nations rage' (Psalm 46:3,4). 'The wicked are like the tossing sea, for it cannot rest' (Isaiah 57:20). The floods of evil are mighty - but the Psalm assures us that God is all-mighty! Yes, 'the floods lift up their roaring', but Yes also, 'Mightier than the thunders of many waters, mightier than the waves of the sea, the Lord on high is mighty.' The message here is that even evil is not outside of God's sway. Evil nations may appear at times to have the upper-hand, but 'He Who sits in heaven laughs; the Lord has them in derision' (Psalm 2:4). Evil is just incapable of dethroning God for 'The Lord has established His throne in the heavens and His kingdom rules over all' (Psalm 103:19). So much for the more 'impersonal' storms, but nearer to home, let us consider the personal storms which we face in our lives.

## THE REALITY OF THE STORMS

Christians are not immune from storms. Christianity is certainly not an insurance against such – in fact it is the universal testimony of believers that problems increase once we are saved. (A friend used to frequent public houses regularly for years, often getting inebriated but never getting thrown out. On conversion he stopped visiting pubs. On revisiting an old drinking den to preach the Gospel however, he promptly got thrown out!)

## THE RULING OF THE SEA

The same, horrendous, stormy incident which occured in the lives of Jesus's disciples is recorded no less than three times in the Gospels (see Matthew 8:23-27; Mark 4:35-41; Luke 8:22-25). It is as though the Holy Spirit would have us sit up and take notice. 'When evening had come, He said to them, "Let us go across to the other side." And leaving the crowd, they took Him with them in the boat, just as He was... And a great storm of wind arose, and the waves beat into the boat, so that the boat was already filling' (Mark 4:36-40).

This incident teaches us much that is applicable to the metaphorical storms which we face in our lives. Notice that the storm came when the disciples were in, not out of the will of God. Jesus had said 'Let us go across to the other side' and the disciples obeyed - and promptly hit a storm! The principle still applies today. Storms are not necessarily a sign of disobedience. Storms are somehow woven into God's overall plan - as any mature Christian will inform us.

Notice also the suddenness of the storm. The Sea of Galilee was notorious for such sudden squalls due to its geographical location funnelling the wind and whipping up the sea. Life too is like that. Sudden storms and calamities appear almost out of nowhere. We never know when unexpected storms and calamities may suddenly hit us. Illness, accident, bereavement, redundancy, disappointment ... all can strike when we are least expecting them. If we are honest, we all have been tempted to say at such times – in unison with those disciples – "Teacher, do you not care if we perish?" (Mark 4:38). This being so, let us allow the happy ending of the incident to burn into our souls. Jesus, remember, was 'in the stern asleep on the cushion' (Mark 4:39). (Before we 'point the finger,' we have to admit that in times of severe storms, we too have been tempted to believe that God does not care, as though He is somehow asleep [Psalm 121:4]). Yet 'He awoke and rebuked the wind, and said to the sea, "Peace! Be still!" And the wind ceased, and there was a great calm' (Mark 4:39). We return to our opening text: 'Mightier than the thunders of many waters, mightier than the waves of the sea, the Lord on high is mighty' (Psalm 93:4) and know that it is true. 'He made the storm be still, and the waves of the sea were hushed. Then they were glad because they had quiet, and He brought them to their desired haven' (Psalm 107:29,30). Harold Paisley comments most helpfully on this whole incident:-

> The raging sea is a picture of the storms of life through which believers are called to pass. Oftentimes the circumstances may be so perplexing that the heart may wonder if the Saviour cares. The compassion of Christ and His control of the situation is encouraging and reassuring ... the violence of the squall did not awaken Him, but the cries of His disciples aroused Him immediately. A mother may sleep through a thunderstorm, but the faintest whimper of her baby instantly awakens her from rest. This is the only record in the Gospel of the Saviour sleeping, yet He interrupted it in the service of others.

## THE REDEMPTION OF THE SAVIOUR

Jesus then, is more powerful than the most powerful storm which we have faced, are facing or ever will face. If we are believers we know this to be the case. Could anything be more powerful and unruly than our sinful hearts? Sin, at its root, is a stubborn and intractable rebellion against God. Yet Jesus has subdued this inner raging of ours; and He has done so because He is the King. The *Shorter Catechism* explains: 'Christ executeth the authority of a King in subduing us to Himself, in ruling and defending us and in restraining and conquering all His and our enemies.' Let us then join with those disciples in the boat, and rejoice in the mighty delivering power of our Mighty Deliverer. 'Those in the boat worshipped Him saying, "Truly you are the Son of God"' (Matthew 14:33).

The storms of our lives are certainly great, fierce and intimidating - but we can be absolutely certain that our God is greater than them all! We should try to think less of our impotence and more of His omnipotence. When storms strike therefore, call out immediately to your Father in heaven. Your testimony too will then be as the Psalmist reported 'This poor man cried, and the Lord heard him, and saved him out of all his troubles' (Psalm 34:6).

If you should ever visit Barry Island, a seaside resort on the South Wales coast, you might notice that Psalm 93:4 has been inscribed on a plaque there, on the headland known as 'Friar's Point.' Underneath the verse is the caption GOD IS ALWAYS GREATER THAN ALL OUR TROUBLES. On a rough, stormy day the text comes home with great force, and we realise that no troubled sea and no troubled soul presents any problem to omnipotence. Another Psalmist wrote similarly of God 'Thou dost rule the raging sea; when its waves rise, Thou stillest them' (Psalm 89:9). When we know that God graciously exerts His omnipotence on our behalf we can make 2 Corinthians 12:9 our own and know with Paul: 'My grace is sufficient for you, for My power is made perfect in weakness' (2 Corinthians 12:9).

# God Cares About You

**Cast all your anxieties of Him, for He cares about you**
**(1 Peter 5:7).**

Worry, anxiety and 'fretting' must be responsible for more deaths than alchohol, terrorism and road accidents combined. Worry ruins our quality of life. Living under the burden of worry and anxiety resembles living under an unseen totalitarian regime - and yet our verse assures the Christian that God's care is such, that we need not live under such a tyranny. Few of us can say with honesty that we never worry, yet a Christian with a furrowed brow verges on a contradiction, as a worried Christian is an implicit denial of God's loving care and sufficiency to provide for all our needs.

## 1. THE LOAD OF CARE : THE WHAT

' ...all your anxieties ...'

1 Peter 5:7 was originally directed to church elders entrusted with the care of souls. Peter himself was one such elder. Where there are people there are problems, and no doubt those early church Pastors knew something of Paul's 'anxiety for all the churches' (2 Corinthians 11:28). Yet the verse has a wider application as well. The verse implies that anxiety is like living under a

heavy burden. 'Anxiety in a man's heart weighs him down' (Proverbs 12:25). We can get anxious about the past, with its failures, regrets and bad memories. We can get anxious about the future with its uncertainties - many of our worries do not actually ever materialise. We can get so anxious about one thousand and one things in the present - health, family, finance, reputation...

Anxiety is a burden. It is carrying a load of care - but Peter exhorts us to cast our burden, whatever it is, on the Lord. He no doubt had Psalm 55:22 in mind when he wrote, 'Cast your burden on the Lord and He will sustain you.'

The word 'all' in our text is all-encompassing. It means that we can literally take 'all' our worries to God and unload them onto Him. This 'all' means that nothing is insignificant in His sight. We can take our little, niggling anxieties to Him as well as the large, devastating ones. God, says Isaiah, 'has weighed the mountains in scales and the hills in a balance' (Isaiah 40:12). This being so, He is well able to bear our burdens! Just as the sea is able to carry a large liner as well as a seagull's feather, so it is with our God and our worries. (Remember that Jesus is described as the One 'upholding the universe by His word of power '[Hebrews 1:3].)

## The Burden Bearer

God then, says our verse, bears our load of care when we unload it upon Him. Interestingly, in the narrow streets of old Jerusalem, even today, you can see a professional burden bearer or 'atal. These men are able to carry absolutely enormous, back-breaking loads, aided only by a knotted rope. I have it on good evidence that some are even able to lift and carry a piano on their backs. In the polite, Middle Eastern society however, it is not unusual to see people passing by and lending a hand to a burden bearer, providing them with welcome relief from their heavy loads. Our text assures us that God is our 'atal. Almighty God Himself lifts our burdens from us and gives us ease.

From the Bible's perspective, sin is our greatest burden. 'My iniquities have gone over my head; they weigh like a burden too heavy for me' says

Psalm 38:4. But on the cross, Christ took this intolerable burden of damning guilt, for 'He Himself bore our sins in His body on the tree' (1 Peter 2:24), or as an alternative reading puts it, 'He Himself carried up our sins in His body to the tree.' An old song goes "Burdens are lifted at Calvary" and it is right! We think again of Christian's load of guilt in *Pilgrim's Progress* and how he unloaded it at the cross:-

> I saw in my dream that just as Christian came up with the cross, his burden loosed off his shoulders, and fell from off his back and began to tumble, and so continued to do, 'till it came to the mouth of the sepulchre where it fell in, and I saw it no more.

Burdens certainly are lifted at Calvary. Jesus said of the Pharisees 'They bind heavy burdens, hard to bear and lay them on men's shoulders' (Matthew 23:4). This contrasts a great deal with Jesus Himself, for He said 'Come to Me all who labour and are heavy laden and I will give you rest ... My yoke is easy and My *burden is light*' (Matthew 11:28-30).

God then takes cares of all our burdens. On the cross He dealt with our greatest burden, the burden of our sin and guilt:-

> *O Christ what burdens bowed Thy head*
> *Our load was laid on Thee*
> *Thou stoodest in the sinner's stead*
> *Didst bear all ill for me*
> *A victim led, Thy blood was shed*
> *Now there's no load for me*

## 2. THE LOVELY COMMAND : THE WAY

'Cast all your anxieties on Him' commands Peter. When I was a boy I remember well the time when we had an extension built on our house. The foundations were dug and a dump loader was filled with rubble. As a special treat I was allowed to accompany one of the builders up to a disposal tip and watch all this rubble being unloaded. The lorry was reversed to the side of the tip, the right button was pressed and the load of rubble was unloaded with a roar.

According to our text, we are to unload our anxieties onto God – and we do so by prayer. John Calvin once said 'Disburden in the bosom of God everything that harasses you.' He may have had Philippians 4:6 in mind:- 'Have no anxiety about anything, but in everything by prayer and supplication with thanksgiving let your requests be made known to God.' It all sounds so basic - but as long as we worry it shows that we have not grasped this basic.

> *Are we weak and heavy laden*
> *Cumbered with a load of care?*
> *Precious Saviour, still our refuge*
> *Take it to the Lord in prayer*
> *Do thy friends despise, forsake thee?*
> *Take it to the Lord in prayer;*
> *In His arms He'll take and shield thee*
> *Thou wilt find a solace there.*

A real life example of the way to unload our care on to God may be evidenced in the life of King Hezekiah in 2 Kings 19. 2 Kings 19 relates how the Assyrians had sent Hezekiah the most threatening of letters. Humanly speaking, it was enough to worry Hezekiah insane. But what did he do? 'Hezekiah went up to the house of the Lord and spread it before the Lord' (2 Kings 19:14). Taking Luke 10:37 out of context, when we have cause to worry we should, 'Go and do likewise.'

## 3. THE LORD'S CONCERN : THE WHY

'He cares about you' Peter assures us, or as another translation puts it 'It matters to Him about you.' We may take both our little and large burdens to God because 'He cares about you' and 'If God is for us, who is against us?' (Romans 8:31). Peter, of course, knew that God cares, as He had lived alongside God's Son for three whole years and seen Him ministering to the needy and heavily burdened at close quarters. Peter had also heard Jesus teach and preach. In emphasising 'He cares about you' Peter was reiterating what Jesus had said during His Sermon on the Mount. Maybe Peter remembered snatches of Jesus's message when He too encouraged His flock with the fact that God's care for our cares enables us to be carefree. Let us hear Jesus's words again on the Galilean hillside. The Saviour too knows how prone we are to worry:-

'Therefore I tell you, do not be anxious about your life, what you shall eat or what you shall drink, nor about your body, what you shall put on. Is not life more than food, and the body more than clothing? Look at the birds of the air: they neither sow nor reap nor gather into barns, and yet your heavenly Father feeds them. Are you not of more value than they? And which of you by being anxious can add one cubit to his span of life? And why are you anxious about clothing? Consider the lilies of the field, how they grow; they neither toil nor spin; yet I tell you, even Solomon in all his glory was not arrayed like one of these. But if God so clothes the grass of the field which today is alive and tomorrow is thrown into the oven, will He not more clothe you, O men of little faith? Therefore do not be anxious, saying 'What shall we eat?' or 'What shall we drink?' or 'What shall we wear?' For the Gentiles seek all these things; and your heavenly Father knows that you need them all. But seek His kingdom and His righteousness, and all these things shall be yours as well. 'Therefore do not be anxious about tomorrow, for tomorrow will be anxious for itself. Let the day's own trouble be sufficient for the day...' (Matthew 6:25-34).

Here Jesus (Who is truth incarnate) argues from the lesser to the greater. His 'theo-logic' is irrrefutable. God cares for the birds and feeds them, He says; God cares for the lilies of the field and clothes them, He says; this being so, how much more does He and will He care for us, who are of such value that we were 'obtained with the blood of His Own Son' (Acts 20:28). Paul argues in a similar way in Romans 8:32 when he reasons 'He Who did not spare His Own Son but gave Him up for us all, will He not also give us all things with Him?' God's giving of His Son to be our Saviour shows that His care for us knows no bounds. A.W. Pink draws out the implications of Romans 8:32 like this:-

> The gift of His own Son, so ungrudgingly and unreservedly bestowed, is the pledge of every needed mercy ... The love that spared not Christ cannot fail its objects nor begrudge any needed blessings ... the one great Gift cost Him much; will He not then bestow the lesser gifts which cost Him nothing but the delight of giving!...

We will need to be reminded of 1 Peter 5:7 continually. Dovetailing as it does with Job 5:7: 'Man is born to trouble as the sparks fly upward,' the reminder will only be unnecessary when we reach the new heavens and the new earth. Let us then, in these worrying days, seek His grace to obey His word, and cast all our anxieties upon Him, knowing in our heart of hearts that our loving heavenly Father really does care, has cared and will take care of all our cares.

*How sweet, my Saviour, to repose*
*On Thine almighty power!*
*To feel Thy strength upholding me*
*Through every trying hour!*

*It is Thy will that I should cast*
*My every care on Thee*
*To Thee refer each rising grief*
*Each new perplexity.*

# The Curse Will Be No More

*There shall no more be anything accursed ...*
*(Revelation 22:3).*

Hope is an essential part of comfort, and only Christians have 'hope' in the true sense of the word. In his glimpse of the glory to come, the aged Apostle John saw in the most enthralling vision that one day God is going to eradicate the curse – and eradicate it totally, absolutely and eternally. Keeping this in mind is the ultimate Christian comfort, for it is only then that our problems, troubles and discomforts will be gone for ever, never to return - the Bible is the only Book which can truly claim the ending 'And they lived happily ever after.'

The last chapter of the New Testament - and so the last chapter of the whole Bible - closes with the comforting news that 'there shall no more be anything accursed' (Revelation 22:3). This is in stark contrast to the last chapter of the Old Testament, as the very last word of the Old Testament is the word curse. Malachi 4:6 completes the Old Testament canon with God Himself warning 'lest I come and smite the land with a *curse.'*

The word 'curse' is one of the most stern and formidable words in the English language. Biblically, it speaks of being under the wrath and judgment of God. Biblically, the worst that could ever happen to anyone would be to hear Jesus say on the Judgment Day 'Depart from Me you *cursed*, into the eternal fire prepared for the devil and his angels' (Matthew 25:41), as this would mean being consigned to eternal hopelessness and torment. The Bible warns us of this final horror often - 'flee from the wrath to come' (Luke 3:7) for 'Jesus ... delivers us from the wrath to come' (1 Thessalonians 1:10).

## 1. THE ENTRANCE OF THE CURSE:
## PARADISE RUINED IN THE GARDEN

God's curse – that is the holy revulsion and reaction of His holy nature against sin – was introduced in the most perfect environment of all, the garden of Eden, Paradise. Adam and Eve knew that God had commanded 'of the tree of the knowledge of good and evil you shall not eat, for in the day that you eat of it you shall die' (Genesis 2:17). (Death - physical, spiritual and eternal - is the judgment of God). We know what ensued only too well. Our first ancestors, succumbing to Satan's suggestion, disobeyed God's command, flouted His authority and ate of the forbidden fruit. God could no more not judge them than He could cease to be God. Immediately following on from this first, seminal sin, God's curse came. Both natural and spiritual harmony were no more and misery entered the stage of life for the first time:-

'The Lord God said to the serpent "Because you have done this, cursed are you above all cattle ..." To the woman He said "I will greatly multiply your pain in child bearing; in pain you shall bring forth children .. ." to Adam He said "cursed is the ground because of you; in toil you shall eat of it ... thorns and thistles it shall bring forth ... In the sweat of your face you shall eat bread ... you are dust and to the dust you shall return ..."' (Genesis 3:14-19).

This event is known as the Fall, and it forms the backcloth to the whole of the Bible's redemptive history. The Bible knows nothing of evolution – devolution is nearer to its world view. The Fall has personal, social and cosmic consequences which are with us now and will only be fully resolved in the Age to come. The Fall brought about a rupture between us and our Maker. The Fall brought in 'nature red in tooth and claw,' – the very next chapter of the Bible (Genesis 4) records the first murder.

The curse of God is the result of sin. Sin began with our first ancestor, and its deadly, deathly and damnable virus has been passed on to every one of his offspring. 'Therefore as sin came into the world through one man and death through sin, and so death spread to all men because all men sinned' (Romans 5:12).

The *Shorter Catechism* states in Q.19:- 'All mankind by their fall lost communion with God, are under His wrath and curse, and so made liable to all miseries in this life, to death itself and to the pains of hell forever.' It is the grim, sober truth.

In Eden, the situation seemed helpless and hopeless to Adam and Eve. The damage they had caused seemed irrepairable and irredeemable. They were just unable to do anything about it in and of themselves – but God in His mercy could. God promised a Redeemer - One to undo the consequences of the Fall and save us from the curse. The Redeemer would undo the destructive damage of Satan and restore the harmony that the creature and Creator once enjoyed. God prophesied to Satan that the Redeemer would be one of the woman's descendants, and so Adam called his wife 'Eve,' meaning 'Living,' as God's promise was a promise of life. Adam believed God's Word spoken to the Enemy of life 'I will put enmity between you and the woman, between your seed and her seed; He shall bruise your head and you shall bruise His heel' (Genesis 3:15).

Living in times A.D., we know that this first Gospel promise was fulfilled in Jesus. 'When the time had fully come, God sent forth His Son, born of woman ... to redeem ... '(Galatians 4:4). To this we now turn. It is the heart of the Gospel, but what we have said so far is a necessary preliminary.

Redemption is meaningless apart from the incident of the Fall as we will only trust the Saviour if we know we are sinners needing to be saved. Also, we will only appreciate 'no more curse' if we know something of the misery and devastation the curse has wrought both personally, socially and cosmically.

## 2. THE EXPIATION OF THE CURSE: PARADISE RECLAIMED AT GOLGOTHA

The curse which is ours was indeed expiated by Christ on the cross. Paradise was indeed reclaimed at Golgotha:-

*My soul looks back to see*
*The burden Christ didst bear*
*When hanging on the cursed tree*
*And knows her guilt was there*

*Believing, we rejoice*
*To see the curse removed*
*We bless the Lamb with cheerful voice*
*And sing His wondrous love*

In a key verse of the Bible, Paul states 'Christ redeemed us from the curse of the law having become a curse for us, for it is written 'cursed be every one who hangs on a tree" (Galatians 3:13). Sin brings guilt which brings God's judgment. Christ, in dying for our sins at Golgotha, both removes our guilt (expiation) and saves us from God's holy wrath and condemnatory judgment (propitiation). The cross then, is the door which re-opens our broken relationship with God. It is the death of Christ on the cross for our sins - and this alone - which restores us to harmony with our Maker. It is the beginning of Paradise reclaimed - the full consummation being in glory.

Galatians 3:13 almost encapsulates the whole of the Christian Faith, the Gospel of redemption. 'Christ redeemed us from the curse of the law having become a curse for us, for it is written 'cursed be every one who hangs on a tree." G.B.Wilson explains:-

> The curse of the law means that every infraction of the law's demand must be visited with the wrath of God, so that in becoming the surety of a sinful people, Christ was made in this respect the object of divine wrath (Matthew 27:46). No words could more clearly express the penal and substitutionary nature of Christ's death. 'Without deliverance from the curse there could be no salvation. It is from this curse that Christ has purchased His people and the price of the purchase was that He Himself became a curse. He became so identified with the curse resting upon His

people that the whole of it in all its unrelieved intensity became His. That curse He bore and that curse He exhausted. That was the price paid for this redemption and the liberty secured for the beneficiaries is that there is no curse' (John Murray).

## 3. THE ERADICATION OF THE CURSE: PARADISE RESTORED IN GLORY

The cross undoes the worst consequence of the curse in that it restores our ruptured relationship with our Maker. However, we know all too well that sin and misery are still with us. The ugly results of the Fall will only be fully eradicated in God's time. 'We wait for new heavens and a new earth in which righteousness dwells' (2 Peter 3:13). 'And the effect of righteousness will be peace, and the result of righteousness quietness and trust for ever ' (Isaiah 32:17). In the new Jerusalem the effects of the curse will have been completely overcome. Zechariah 14:11 will be fulfilled:- 'there shall be no more curse.'

### Cosmic Redemption

The cross - as every Christian knows - has the most blessed spiritual results, saving our souls from God's curse, and so enabling us to enjoy the fellowship with Him for which we were designed. But how little the cosmic results of the cross are emphasised - 'and through Him to reconcile to Himself all things, whether on earth or in heaven, making peace by the blood of His cross' (Colossians 1:20).

We are saved now spiritually, but one day, salvation will be both bodily and cosmic as well. We will be redeemed in both soul and body to enjoy God's presence for ever in the new heavens and the new earth. It is only then that Paradise will be completely restored and the finished Work of Christ fully and finally consummated. The Fall has affected the whole creation. Thorns and thistles, death and decay are familiar parts of our scene – but these are not for ever. 'The creation was subjected to futility not of its own will but by the will of Him Who subjected it in hope; because creation itself will be set free from its bondage to decay and obtain the glorious liberty of the children of God' (Romans 8:20,21).

It is difficult for us, in this war-torn, cruel and brutal world, even to begin to conceive of the perfect harmony there will be in the new heavens and the new earth. What must it be like to be incapable of sinning! Maybe that is why John states it in the negative - 'there shall no more be anything accursed.' Isaiah however does dare to describe something of the wonders of the cosmic redemption to come. In figurative language he relates:-

> '... they shall beat their swords into ploughshares, and their spears into pruning hooks; nation shall not lift up sword against nation, neither shall they learn war any more' (Isaiah 2:4).
> 'The wolf shall dwell with the lamb, and the leopard shall lie down with the kid, and the calf and the lion and the fatling together, and a little child shall lead them. The cow and the bear shall feed; their young shall lie down together; and the lion shall eat straw like the ox. The sucking child shall play over the hole of the asp, and the weaned child shall put his hand on the adder's den. They shall not hurt or destroy in all my holy mountain; for the earth shall be full of the knowledge of the Lord as the waters cover the sea ' (Isaiah 11:6-9).

Afflicted Christian, take heart! The best is yet to be. Our present trials will be nothing in comparison with our coming eternal bliss. The day is certainly coming when all tears will be dried and all hurts will be healed. God is going to destroy the curse completely. Be assured therefore, that no matter how hard the present may be, 'this slight momentary affliction is preparing for us an eternal weight of glory beyond comparison' (2 Corinthians 4:17).

# The Night Will Be No More

*... there shall be no night there*
**(Revelation 21:25).**

For the Christian, the best is yet to be. Heaven is the land of endless day, and it is to this land we are heading by God's grace in Jesus Christ. In heaven all darkness - physical, moral and spiritual - will be banished finally, utterly, completely and eternally. In heaven we will bask in the light of God's glory forevermore.

Heaven will never hear the following prayer being uttered:- 'Lift up the light of Thy countenance upon us O Lord' (Psalm 4:6), just as in heaven we will not have to pray 'lead us not into temptation, but deliver us from evil' (Matthew 6:13). Such requests will be blessedly redundant in our Home of eternal light.

*There is a Home eternal*
*Beautiful and bright*
*Where sweet joys supernal*
*Never are dimmed by night*
*White robed angels are singing*
*Ever around the bright throne*
*When, oh, when shall I see thee*
*Beautiful, beautiful Home.*

The fear of darkness is universal, but this fear was much more apparent in biblical times before electricity and gas had been discovered. In biblical times oil and wicks were the means of banishing darkness, and so we read that one of the good woman's virtues in Proverbs 31 was to ensure 'her lamp does not go out at night' (Proverbs 31:18). James M. Freeman in *Manners and Customs of the Bible* comments:-

> To the ... mind of the Oriental, light is an object of desire and darkness something to be greatly dreaded. The lamp is usually kept burning in the house all night, and its light is used as an emblem of prosperity, and the extinguishment of it as an emblem of great calamity (cf Revelation 18:23). (p.210).

What music to the ears of John's original readers then was the message that in glory 'night shall be no more' (Revelation 22:5) - and what a welcome assurance to us too, as we shall now see:-

## 1. HEAVEN IS THE PLACE OF GOD'S IMMEDIATE PRESENCE

There can be no night in heaven as heaven is God's special dwelling place, and 'God is light and in Him is no darkness at all ' (1 John 1:5). In heaven 'night shall be no more; they need no light of lamp or sun, for the Lord God will be their light, and they shall reign for ever' (Revelation 22:5). In heaven we will meet our wonderful Saviour face to face. Then we will realise afresh the truth of the claim He once made on earth:- 'I am the light of the world; he who follows Me will not walk in darkness but will have the light of life' (John 8:12). God's presence and night are incompatible - but what a stark contrast is this joy to the hell of God's absence. Hell is described by Jesus in terms of 'the outer darkness; there men will weep and gnash their teeth' (Matthew 8:12).

## 2. HEAVEN IS THE PLACE OF FULL SALVATION

Biblically, the Christian answer to the question 'Are you saved?' is 'I am saved, I am being saved and I will be saved.' The last will only be fulfilled in the land of 'no night.' As full salvation means dwelling in eternal light, it comes as no surprise to see that the Bible frequently describes our present salvation in similar terms: Christ 'abolished death and brought life and immortality to light through the Gospel' (2 Timothy 1:10). Paul reminded the Ephesian believers 'once you were darkness, but now you are light in the Lord' (Ephesians 5:8) and likewise the Thessalonians 'you are all sons of light and sons of the day; we are not of the night or of darkness' (1 Thessalonians 5:5). Peter similarly exhorts us to 'declare the wonderful deeds of Him Who called you out of darkness into His glorious light' (1 Peter 2:9). Paradise will be the completion, culmination and consummation of these glorious realities. God's salvation means 'He has delivered us from the dominion of darkness and transferred us to the kingdom of His beloved Son' (Colossians 1:13), and these realities, both present and future, should have a positive effect on our current behaviour for 'the night is far gone, the day is at hand. Let us then cast off the works of darkness and put on the armour of light' (Romans 13:12).

## 3. HEAVEN WILL SEE THE END OF THE NIGHT OF TROUBLE AND SORROW

Life on earth, even for the Christian, has many dark moments. If you have not already experienced these, it is unlikely that you would be reading this book. Sorrow, pain, perplexity, grief, sudden calamity ... are part and parcel of life in this fallen world. We sympathise with the hymnwriter:-

*Days of darkness still come o'er me*
*Sorrow's path I often tread*
*But the Saviour still is with me*
*By His hand I'm safely led.*

Suffering Job articulated the heart of suffering Everyman when he cried out in the midst of his anguish:- 'He has set darkness upon my paths' (Job 19:8), and 'nights of misery are apportioned to me ... the night is long' (Job 7:3,4). Our text then comes as a great solace to us all. 'There shall be no night' (Revelation 21:25), for 'He shall wipe away every tear from their eyes, and death shall be no more, neither shall there be mourning nor pain any more, for the former things have passed away' (Revelation 21:4).

## 4. HEAVEN WILL SEE THE END OF THE NIGHT OF EVIL AND FEAR

The Bible undoubtedly contains parts that are difficult to understand, but its expression 'the terror of the night' (Psalm 91:5) presents no such difficulty. Night-time can be fearful. Much evil is done under the cover of darkness. Paul used the expression 'a thief in the night' (1 Thessalonians 5:2) to describe the effect of the Second Coming on the unsaved. Locking our doors at night is so routine we do it automatically. It is a way of restraining evil and calming our fears. Jesus said that one characteristic of the unregenerate is that they 'loved darkness rather than light because their deeds were evil' (John 3:19). Crime being what it is, we have good reason to be afraid of the night, just as they did in biblical times. 'Thou makest darkness, and it is night, when all the beasts of the forest creep forth' (Psalm 104:20). This world has so many dark and dangerous aspects to it. They fill us with fear.

Paradise however will see the complete end to all evil, danger and fear. You will notice with relief that unrepentant murderers are on the list of those excluded from heaven (Revelation 21:8); but more positively, heaven will know no fear, as in heaven we will bask in the presence of the God Who is perfect love. 'There is no fear in love, but perfect love casts out fear' (1 John 4:18). In heaven we will be both eternally saved and eternally safe.

## 5. HEAVEN WILL SEE AN END TO THE NIGHT OF PERPLEXITY

We sometimes say when we do not know something "I'm in the dark on the matter," and we sometimes ask "Can you shed any light on this?" Christians are blessed above all others in that they have the light of God's Word to give help and guidance in this world which is stumbling in the dark. 'Thy Word is a lamp to my feet and a light to my path' (Psalm 119:105). The light of God's Word notwithstanding however, much on earth can leave us very puzzled and perplexed. We have so many unanswered questions. We are 'in the dark' about so much, not least over the problem of suffering... "Why was my child born handicapped?" "Why was my son killed so brutally?" "Why has my husband gone senile?" "Why can't I get a job?" "Why was I confined to being single all my days?"...Why why why...? Faith involves trusting God in the dark, and living by His promises and not by explanations. Jesus once said 'What I am doing you do not know now, but afterward you will understand' (John 13:7), and we can apply this to all the suffering which God permits to come our way. God is under no obligation to explain His ways to us. He is God and not man, His ways are infinitely higher, above and beyond ours. We are the clay, and He is the potter - but in heaven all will be made plain. 'For now we see in a mirror dimly, but then face to face. Now I know in part; then I shall understand fully, even as I have been fully understood' (1 Corinthians 13:12).

> *Not 'till the loom is silent*
> *And the shuttles cease to fly*
> *Shall God unroll the canvas*
> *And explain the reason why*
> *The dark threads are as needful*
> *In the weaver's skillful hand*
> *As the threads of gold and silver*
> *In the pattern He has planned.*

In the meantime, it is incumbent upon us to cleave to what God has actually revealed in His Word. 'You will do well to pay attention to this as to a lamp shining in a dark place until the day dawns and the morning star rises in your hearts' (2 Peter 1:19).

## 6. HEAVEN WILL KNOW NOTHING OF THE DARKNESS OF GOD'S JUDGMENT

Hell's outer darkness and exclusion from the light of God's presence is the ultimate in judgment - and it is eternal, with no way out. Darkness, in the Bible, often symbolises God's fearful wrath. "'And on that day," says the Lord God, "I will make the sun go down at noon, and *darken*the earth in broad daylight."' (Amos 8:9). 'A day of wrath is that day, a day of distress and anguish, a day of ruin and devastation, a day of *darkness* and gloom, a day of clouds and thick *darkness*' (Zephaniah 1:15).

The Bible however assures believers that 'There is therefore now no condemnation for those who are in Christ Jesus' (Romans 8:1) and that 'there shall be no night there' in glory. We can be sure that these realities are blessedly true because Jesus was condemned in our place. This is an historical fact. Jesus took upon Himself the darkness of God's wrath so that we might dwell in eternal light. 'Sending His Own Son in the likeness of sinful flesh and for sin He condemned sin in the flesh' (Romans 8:3). It really happened. At Calvary Jesus tasted hell's darkness to bring all who believe in Him to heaven's light. In surely some of the most formidable verses of Scripture we read what happened: 'Now from the sixth hour there was *darkness* over all the land until the ninth hour. And about the ninth hour Jesus cried with a loud voice, "Eli, Eli, lama sabachthani?" that is "My God, my God, why hast Thou forsaken Me?"' (Matthew 27:45,46).

There really will be no night in heaven. What a comfort this is to us who live in this world which can be so dark, dingy, dreary, dismal and devastating. But are any of us really fit for the light of glory? If we know anything of our own hearts, we cannot but be aware of the darkness lurking even in a regenerate heart. The Gospel of Jesus Christ however assures even the darkest sinner of a home in the eternal light. The following lesser known hymn makes this clear, and with this we conclude our meditation on the glorious prospect that in glory the 'night shall be no more' (Revelation 22:5).

*Eternal light! Eternal light!*
*How pure the soul must be*
*When placed within Thy searching sight*
*It shrinks not but with calm delight*
*Can live and look on Thee*

*O how shall I, whose native sphere*
*Is dark whose mind is dim*
*Before the Ineffable appear*
*And on my naked spirit bear*
*The uncreated beam?*

*There is a way for man to rise*
*To that sublime abode*
*An offering and a sacrifice*
*A Holy Spirit's energies*
*An Advocate with God*

*There, these prepare us for the sight*
*Of holiness above*
*The sons of ignorance and night*
*Can dwell in the eternal light*
*Through the eternal love*

'Yea ... the Lord my God lightens my darkness' (Psalm 18:3).

# The Sea Will Be No More

*Then I saw a new heaven and a new earth; for the first*
*heaven and the first earth had passed away*
*and the sea was no more*
**(Revelation 21:1).**

John's glimpse of the eternal glory on the Isle of Patmos revealed many strange and wonderful things. We have seen so far that in the new heavens and the new earth there will be no more curse and no more night. But this verse - given to John when he was surrounded by the sea - reveals that in the eternal state the sea will actually be no more.

If I may be personal, I love the sea. I can well do without both the curse and the night, but the sea? These words are actually being written a mere five minutes walk from the sea, and living here is most congenial. Watching the sun sink into the horizon or watching the spray fly on a rough day are thrilling privileges. How sad then that, according to our verse, the redeemed will, in God's time, never see the ocean again - but actually it is not so sad when we consider just what the sea meant to the minds of those living in the Bible's day.

## 1. THE SEA OF DANGER

Whilst most of us here in Great Britain enjoy the sea, many do not. Those who work on the sea are well aware of just how dangerous it can be. Storms of course are the obvious danger, but then there are the more subtle dangers of hidden rocks and reefs. You can set sail, even on a calm day, but nevertheless get dashed upon hidden rocks and be shipwrecked. When we think of the sea we may also think of wars. Many battles have been fought and an incalculable number of lives lost by war at sea. How comforting then that John saw 'the sea was no more.'

Sailing on the sea of life also has its dangers. We can be sailing along so smoothly – and then suddenly hit a storm. We may also have seen others make a total shipwreck of their life and faith, and it acts as a stern warning. Life also contains hidden rocks and reefs – hidden dangers and devastations. Who knows where you and I may be even this time next week? We could be dashed on the as yet hidden rocks of illness, disappointment, disaster ... Life is so dangerous and uncertain. Living amidst 'the troubles' of N. Ireland certainly brought this home; the expression "DV" (God Willing) took on a new reality there – but wherever we live we are exposed to danger, be it physical, psychological, moral or spiritual. The last three can hurt even more than the first. Being laughed and sneered at, or being let down by a friend can hurt us inside very deeply, as can be being mocked for our Faith. Thankfully there will be no such danger in our eternal Home, when 'the sea was no more.' There all woes, wars and worries will be banished eternally.

## 2. THE SEA OF DECAY

If you were to go down to the sea early, you could watch the tide roll in. If you were to stay long enough, you could watch the tide roll out - and then in again. Twice a day, every day, in and out comes the tide. Time rolls on. The days pass by. We grow older, we lose our vigour, we decay. . .

John knew all about old age. He was perhaps ninety years old when he wrote our text. When we are first introduced to John he was probably in his 'teens. See him out-running Peter in John chapter 20! But by now age had set in ... even his grey hair had turned white ... arthritis was in his joints ... Old age can be rather ugly. Old peoples' homes can be somewhat depressing places – especially if you visit someone you have known in their more vigorous prime. It is heartbreaking to see a loved one lose their mind and eventually become so senile that they do not even give you a glimmer of recognition. How welcome to know then that there will be no more sea of age, infirmity and decay in glory. 'The sea was no more.' In glory, time will have gone and eternity will have arrived. It is impossible for us to conceive of this now, limited as we are by time and space . In glory though:-

*When we've been there ten thousand years*
*Bright shining as the sun*
*We've no less days to sing God's praise*
*Than when we've first begun.*

## 3. THE SEA OF DEPRAVITY

In the Eastern mind-set, the sea was not associated with images of pleasure, as it might be in the modern West. Isaiah tells us 'the wicked are like the tossing sea; for it cannot rest, and its waters toss up mire and dirt' (Isaiah 57:20). Jude wrote of the wicked who were like 'wild waves of the sea, casting up the foam of their own shame' (Jude 13). Earlier in his vision, John had written 'I saw a beast rising out of the sea, with ten horns and seven heads, with ten diadems upon its horns and a blasphemous name upon its heads' (Revelation 13:1). How totally restless evil seems to be in this world. The very next news broadcast can make us shudder to the core. How good then, that in glory 'the sea was no more' and this world's restless wickedness will give way to perfect peace. Evil will then be no more as the Devil will have been forever routed. John explained this in his previous chapter:- 'the Devil who had deceived them was thrown into the lake of fire and sulphur where the beast and the false prophet were, and they will be tormented day and night forever' (Revelation 20:10).

We only have to take a walk down the street to see the ravages that depravity brings. Nothing much has changed since Cain murdered Abel. If we are honest though, we have only to look inside our own hearts to know that the seeds of heinous sins are within us. Even regenerate Christians are capable of commiting the most degenerate acts. The Bible exhorts us to be watchful. No one is immune from temptation - not even a Christian. But we are promised 'The sea was no more.' There will be no more evil without or within in the glory of heaven, for God will have dried up the sea of depravity for ever.

## 4. THE SEA OF DAMNATION

The sea also speaks of God's judgment. Way back in the days of Noah we read 'the Lord saw that the wickedness of man was great in the earth, and that every imagination of the thoughts of his heart was only evil continually' (Genesis 6:5). We all know what happened. 'God said to Noah, "I have determined to make an end of all flesh ... I will bring a flood of waters upon the earth, to destroy all flesh in which is the breath of life from heaven"' (Genesis 6:13,17).

So we see here the sea of damnation – '. . . the world that then existed was deluged with water and perished' (2 Peter 3:6). It was fearful - but if we are saved we need have no such fear. In glory, we will never fear the judgment of God for our sins, but not because we are sinless. Far from it. We need not fear the judgment of God for our sins because Jesus was condemned in our place. The sea speaks of the wrath of God, and when Jesus died on the cross He took the full force of this stormy judgment to save us from perishing eternally. The following Scriptures seem to picture Christ's death on the cross, when He averted the sea of God's wrath:-

'all Thy waves and billows have gone over Me' (Psalm 42:7),

'Thy wrath lies heavy upon Me and Thou dost overwhelm Me with Thy waves' (Psalm 88:7).

It is true then, just as it will be true, that 'there is therefore now no condemnation to those who are in Christ Jesus' (Romans 8:1). Glory will know nothing of the sea of God's wrath. 'The sea was no more.'

*The tempest's awful voice was heard*
*O Christ it broke on Thee*
*Thy open bosom was my ward*
*It braved the storm for me*
*Thy form was scarred, Thy visage marred*
*Now cloudless peace for me*

## 5. THE SEA OF DIVISION

The sea of division will also be eradicated in the day when 'the sea was no more.' The Apostle John was well aware that the ocean divides. On the Isle of Patmos he was separated from his beloved flock in Ephesus, and it no doubt hurt. When I lived in N. Ireland, I too did not appreciate the Irish Sea separating me from my family in Wales - as now I do not appreciate the Irish Sea keeping me from my friends in N. Ireland! Oceans certainly do divide - but there will be no such division in heaven. Earthly separation will give way to eternal reconciliation when 'the sea was no more.'

The Gospel is all about reconciliation. Sin separates us from God, but the Gospel proclaims 'God was in Christ reconciling the world to Himself not counting their trespasses against them' (2 Corinthians 5:19). Here on earth, our standing before God can never be shaken, but our fellowship with Him can. Sin can still come in between us and our Maker. John had written previously to Christians 'If we say we have no sin we deceive ourselves and the truth is not in us. If we confess our sins He is faithful and just and will forgive our sins and cleanse us from all unrighteousness' (1 John 1:8,9). Until we die, such daily confession of our sins will be compulsory if we are to enjoy unbroken fellowship with God. Glory, however, will be the place of unhindered fellowship with both our Maker and our fellow creatures. Sin will not divide us then. Even the best of earthly Christian fellowships can be spoilt by sin and separate off and sub-divide into cliques. In glory though, these seas of division will be gone forever - heaven will know nothing of Christian denominations. Heaven, to anticipate, will also know no death. Death is the ultimate divider. The joy of re-uniting with loved ones will be greater than words can tell. So let us now consider:-

## 6. THE SEA OF DEATH

Unless the Lord returns, death will one day swallow us all up. It is one of the few certainties of life - yet John informs us that one day this sea will be gone.

It is imperative that people are rescued quickly when they have been thrown into the water in disasters at sea. Even in the hottest climate the ocean is very cold, and hypothermia soon sets in as the body temperature is lowered by the icy sea.

Death too is an icy cold experience. Not only is the body cold when life has left it, but death also brings a coldness to the hearts of those left behind. At such a time we realise just how cold and frosty this world really is. It cannot help us at all - only the love of God can thaw our frozen hearts.

The sea of death, the greatest of all 'swallowers', is surely the coldest sea of all - but one day it will be no more. Christianity is all about eternal *life*. One day, if we are Christ's, we will shout 'Death is swallowed up in victory.' 'O death where is thy victory? O death, where is thy sting?' (1 Corinthians 15:54,55). 'The wages of sin is death', yes, 'but the free gift of God is eternal life in Christ Jesus our Lord' (Romans 6:23). It is the death and resurrection of Jesus which assures us that we will never perish in the icy sea of spiritual death. '. . . our Saviour Christ Jesus ... abolished death and brought life and immortality to light through the Gospel' (2 Timothy 1:10). It is small wonder that Paul brings his triumphant 'resurrection chapter' to a climax with 'thanks be to God, Who gives us the victory through our Lord Jesus Christ' (1 Corinthians 15:57). He surely does. Finally, let us consider:-

## 7. THE SEA OF DELIGHT

'The sea was no more', John assures. Paradoxically though, Revelation also informs us that there *is* a sea in glory. 'Before the throne there is, as it were, a sea of glass like crystal' (Revelation 4:6); and Revelation 15:2 records the redeemed 'standing beside the sea of glass with harps of God in their hands.' We have to be careful when considering Revelation's symbolism, (Revelation has perhaps suffered more from far-fetched misinterpretation than any other book in the Book), but we can compare Scripture with Scripture to aid our understanding. Here, the heavenly imagery of the 'sea of glass' seems to be patterned on the earthly tabernacle and temple, described earlier on in the Bible.

God instructed Moses 'You shall make a laver of bronze, with its base of bronze for washing' (Exodus 30:17). We read too of the temple 'Then he made the molten sea;... it held two thousand baths' (1 Kings 7:23 ff). Both of these 'seas' were positioned before the Holy Place, and used for ritual purification. They speak of the needed purity if we are ever to approach a holy God. This in turn speaks loudly of the work of the Lord Jesus Christ.

The purity which God requires is the purity which He has provided for us in Christ – '. . . the washing of regeneration ' (Titus 3:5). Calvary alone makes us fit for heaven for 'Christ loved the Church and gave Himself up for her, having cleansed her by the washing of the water with the Word' (Ephesians 5:26). '. . . you were washed . . .' (1 Corinthians 6:11). And so in glory, standing by the 'sea of glass', we will be reminded of Calvary's 'fountain for sin and unclean-ness' (Zechariah 13:1) for all eternity. There in our new, sinless bodies, living in a perfect sinless environment, we will be able to give to our God our more perfect praise for His saving, cleansing, heaven-fitting love in Jesus Christ. 'The sea was no more' : 'the sea of glass'. All because of the love of Jesus, the only lasting comfort we can or will ever have.

*Oh the deep deep love of Jesus*
*Vast unmeasured boundless free*
*Rolling as a mighty ocean*
*In its fullness over me*
*Underneath me all around me*
*is the current of Thy love*
*Leading onward leading homeward*
*To my glorious home above.*

**SOLI DEO GLORIA**

# Epilogue

Almighty and Everlasting God,
The comfort of the sad;
The strength of the sufferers;
Let the prayers of those that cry
Out of tribulation, come unto Thee;
That all may rejoice, to find
That Thy mercy is present
With them in their afflictions;
Through Jesus Christ our Lord,
Amen

(Taken from the Church of Ireland Common Prayer Book,
with thanks to Sir James Molyneux M.P.).